ERIN JAMES

Feral

"The Art of Creating Success Without Permission."

First edition

ISBN: 9798990593909

This book was professionally typeset on Reedsy.
Find out more at reedsy.com

Contents

Introduction

Praise

"Since Erin James has entered the yarn scene, she has hit the ground running with an unparalleled energy and uncompromising work ethic. She fearlessly shares everything she learns with others and provides resources for spinners around the world. Erin is an ideas machine, authentic and unapologetic about her space in the community, witty and vibrant - she makes the learning curve of spinning yarn joyful and exciting. She's the fiber friend who embraces the mess, puts her family first, tells you the whole truth, does hard things for breakfast, hugs you when you're ugly crying, and stands her ground on her values. She is ruthlessly generous and her honesty and perspective create a community atmosphere wherever she goes. I'm so proud of the work she has put into this book and look forward to seeing what mountains she climbs next."

Ashley Martineau
Neauveau

"Working with Erin made me realize how much greater my own indie business could be. It doesn't need to just be a side hustle. She taught me that our craft could and should be the main gig. I am forever grateful for her."

Heidi Stone Black
Cocoon Homespun Goods

Erin James is truly a force to be reckoned with. Her creativity knows no bounds, drawing you into her world and instantly making you feel like part of something greater. She has an insatiable curiosity for all things yarn and is a wonderful teacher — encouraging you to dive deep down the rabbit hole as you explore your own passions. What sets Erin apart is her unwavering support for small, independent, and women-owned businesses, up-lifting everyone in her path. Collaborating with her over the years has been an absolute joy, leaving me constantly inspired and dreaming of future opportunities to work together again.

Jessica Ays
Double the Stitches

"This is exactly the kind of tongue in cheek wisdom that I wish I had when I was first starting out. Erin's story is such an inspiration no matter where you currently are in your business journey"

Dawn Prickett, founder of Twice Sheared Sheep

Introduction

I always thought I would have something worth-while to pass on once I was done accomplishing and living things, but it turns out that you just have to start. So many of us grew up thinking that success was a destination that we would eventually achieve. I know that personally, I had visions of myself, somehow taller and more polished than I actually am, wearing business clothes that people would take seriously and making decisions that people respected. In my imagination, I was a college professor or academic. I would have a job title and a desk in an office, where I would help people and have interesting, useful ideas and write lots of papers. People would think I was really getting somewhere and contributing, and my family would be proud.

I remember having this fantasy about my future self, and of course, I would be madly in love, married, and would have children because I always wanted to have a family. In my fantasy, my kids would somehow be in super affordable part-time daycare, and I would somehow be working and having all of these important thoughts while my kids were being looked after by somebody truly amazing who wasn't too expensive. I would somehow be able to divide my thoughts and my time between being a mom, a wife, and an academic who is well respected, all while wearing stylish, appropriate clothing with good hair. If this is you and you are somehow already living this life and you want to raise your hand and inform me that you actually can live that way, then this book is definitely not for you. You have somehow surpassed me and reached a level that

I have not yet unlocked. However, if you are either starting out or already stuck somewhere along the way and kind of pissed off about it, then this book might just fit.

As an elder millennial, I feel like my entire life there has been this discussion about how women could have it all and what that would even look like, what the virtues of having it all would be. I felt like there was always this question hanging over everyone's head: were you going to work or were you going to stay home with your children? I personally thought this was super unfair because why couldn't you just do both? That's what everybody tries to do, it seems. We all try to do both, but what no one tells you is that both can look really different for everyone, and depending on how you look at it, it can either be incredibly unfulfilling, disappointing, and leave you lost and depressed, or if you take charge of your own reality, it can be the most freeing experience ever.

If you have a professional career, the path before you is typically clearer and more defined. I have friends who have professional careers, and I am incredibly proud and impressed by them. However, I am writing this for women like myself, entrepreneurial by nature, but with many different facets of personality that must be considered.

People often label us as dysfunctional daydreamers, lazy, or unfocused. Others see the passion and unrealistic moments of our impulsive nature, but they don't always understand who we really are.

Like the good anthropologist I am, I have thoroughly observed, researched, and recorded how to remake myself as the person who is living the life I wanted. It can be easier to change yourself into the person who gets to walk out the happiness you crave than it is to stay on a constant journey toward a nameless destination that you dreamed up.

There is a lot you have to let go of and hold on to. There is a lot you can't control, but there is also so much more that you can control and change than you realize. The options are endless while the answers are also simple. We have so much creative freedom thanks to technology, but there is so much wisdom to be gained from looking at our own nature and deep-rooted truths.

1

Origin story

After college, I followed the traditional path and took jobs related to my degrees, but I also took many uninspiring ones just to make money. During this time, my long-time boyfriend and I moved from Charleston, SC to Eastern WA. Both of us were struggling to get started with our careers.

Like most people of our generation, we graduated from college just in time for the 2008 recession, and literally everything came crashing down. However, we have been incredibly blessed to find success, largely due to taking a chance and moving cross-country. Having children was a significant change, and I had to learn how to be myself all over again. What people do not tell you about having kids is that you can feel a lingering sadness where you mourn the death of your previous life or self. Then you feel guilty because you wouldn't trade this child for anything in the entire universe. You can love your children so much it'll make your eyes cross, but that doesn't make anything easier. Like many moms, it was tough for me to know how to fit into my own skin, let alone society's idea of what I should be.

When I was pregnant with my first daughter, I couldn't picture myself as a mom. I was determined that I was just going to be myself, exactly as I was, but with a baby. It stressed me out to no end when people would tell me that a baby was going to "change everything." I loved my life and worked hard on dieting, working out, and having a nice life. I did not want to change. It turns out they were right, of course, but I still wish they hadn't kept saying it because the more they said it, the more I was determined not to change. I held onto my old life, clothes, and expectations like my life depended on it. Losing touch with the person I had been felt like my identity was at stake. This resistance to change hurt, and for around five years, I felt like a weird, pale ghost of myself.

During that time, I had my second daughter (basically back to back), and we moved cross-country again to Knoxville, TN for my husband's work and to be closer to family. During this time, I had gotten back into my college pastime of knitting and, later, spinning my own yarn. I started a small Etsy shop selling hats and other items and discovered that making even $20 made me happy. I had always wanted to run my own business, but dreaming of entrepreneurial success in high school looked like taking out a bank loan to open a brick-and-mortar shop, and that always seemed too big and scary to achieve. I had the entrepreneurial itch but had zero know-how or an example to follow. I set out to learn everything I could about ranking on Etsy. My dad and husband had both had good luck selling things on eBay over the years, so I felt like Etsy would be the handmade version I needed. If I could crack the code, I'd be in business.

I started with what seemed like a simple enough question: "How do you sell on Etsy?"

The answer wasn't easy. There are over 40 million sellers on Etsy, and more who will be joining them soon—there are only so many search results you can show at once, so it made sense that there were some tricks of the trade for getting your products to stand out above all the rest.

Even though I have all but abandoned Etsy at this point and don't really recommend it for selling (due to the market being flooded with not really handmade items but mostly the crazy fees they keep dumping on sellers), through this research, I was able to find many online mentors and information that helped me set a good foundation for building my own business independent of Etsy's search engine.

I found out that there are many different ways you can make money with your crafts and ideas. You just need to find the right one that fits your skillset, time availability, budget, and passion.

I discovered early on that I really wanted to sell hand-spun yarn (and later spinning fiber and supplies). I loved the process and the fact that each piece seemed to be its own humble little piece of usable art. With a background in fine art galleries and sales, this one-of-a-kind approach really appealed to me, and I thought it would be a great niche to try to fill online.

When I first started thinking about this project, I had a lot of ideas. I thought that if I could make a website, I could then sell hand-spun yarn to people all over the world. As I started digging around on

Google, I found that there weren't very many sites devoted to selling hand-spun yarn. Most of them were on Etsy.

I decided that this would be my calling: if only I could make a designer-looking website and then learn how to rank on Google, surely the sales would start pouring in!

I've since found out that pretty much any great vision you have for what you're trying to do is only partly right—you have to get knee-deep into it before you can really see where the firm ground is, and by then you've probably altered the original idea by at least a few degrees. That will be a lesson for a later chapter.

While building what I hoped would become the fine art gallery of the hand-spun yarn world (a website dedicated to celebrating this unique craft), we also picked up and moved from WA, back towards our Southern roots. This is how we landed in Knoxville, TN. This was a monumental undertaking, as you can imagine, with two small children and a husband working what seemed like constantly at a new position. This is why I so strongly feel that family life and marriage can't really be 50/50. I really think if you can work together and trust each other enough to be 100/100 and flexible, you'll have more peace and, hopefully, prosperity. Even though I didn't realize it, having my "silly little website" that I could build and then put on hold during this trying time gave me the flexibility (and hope for a future where I actually got to have a project I would enjoy) and motivation that I needed to not sink into too much stress and depression. I had something to look forward to. Something I could do on my own time and with very little effort. Something that, if it didn't work out, gave me the freedom to just throw it away and not feel bad about it. It was a small project, but it was mine. For some people, decorating a new house or throwing themselves into becoming the queen of preschool activities may have filled that void, but I wanted something that felt more like a business. I've always loved making money – it's like the ultimate game to me. I love figuring out some way to turn $1 into $2 and then use that money to do whatever the hell I wanted. Money has always been the freedom that I wanted – the freedom to live my life like I want and spend money on dumb stuff the kids and I wanted without thinking about it. Money, to me, equaled being able to decorate my new house and do all the fun little kid stuff. I wanted to use my time to build something so that I then had the freedom to do what I wanted. We are very blessed that my husband has always provided incredibly well for us, no matter what season we were in, but no matter how much "household" money there is, there is always that little thrill of having that extra that you know isn't affecting the household income at all. Later in this book, I will discuss the reasons why I think that the Internet has created a unique opportunity for women to establish themselves as entrepreneurs. The "coffee can" money – as our grandmothers might have called it – is an option open to more and more people who want balanced lives. My business has grown from just handspun yarn and a few knitted items to collections of beautiful fibers, as well as spinning wheels, digital content, and monthly subscriptions. I have developed a growing business that allows me flexibility and the ability to be home with my children, while still earning an income. I am not alone. Thousands of women around the world are starting small businesses that support their families and create opportunities for themselves. Now, please don't picture that all of a sudden things blew up and I was flooded with all of this money and success. To me, that's how it always seemed when you would hear of other people's success. For me, it was just lots of little decisions to try new things like subscriptions and just figure it out on the way. It's been a lot of growth and then spending to support the growth. Adding team members and then freaking out that I'm now "the boss". The daily struggle of still identifying to myself and others as "a stay-at-home mom" or "I have a little yarn business".

It was always funny when I would be introduced to new people and they would ask, "What do I do?" When you work for yourself at home, your personal and work life is so complexly intertwined it's basically impossible to answer this. I would have the WORST case of imposter syndrome ever, so saying anything that wasn't shuffling my feet and making it sound insignificant was next to impossible.

I went from "I have an ETSY Shop" to "I have a Yarn business" (no one knows what the fiber arts is) to "I run websites in the fiber arts world" and then landed somewhere around "I work in marketing and promotion for small indie businesses." That last one is probably the most accurate because I own Feral Scene LLC, which umbrellas "Crafty Housewife Yarns" and "My Local Wool", and I was also hired as the marketing and social media director for SpinOlution Spinning Wheels, for which I had been a long-time top dealer. My contracted employees handle most of the "making" these days, and I really do mainly content creation, writing, filming, posting, and scheduling for three different brands. I have learned that as you grow, what you do changes – you have to learn to become the boss and then the owner much more than the worker or artist. I have taken back my creating for my own enjoyment and a subscription here and there. The label "entrepreneur" has a special place in my heart because it's not a job description so much as a calling or sickness, depending on how you look at it. Entrepreneur is a personality trait, a quirk, and a way of being. I always joke that I absolutely could never go back to working retail at the mall, folding sweaters and trading my time and life for an hourly wage. If my business fell through, you'd find me selling high-end foot pictures on OnlyFans or something equally silly, but on my own terms, before you'd find me working hourly on someone else's schedule. I have immense respect for the hard workers, the individuals living the life of luxury, and everyone in between, who have mastered the art of leveraging their authenticity for success.

This is my internal rant most days when I hear women bemoaning having it all. Working themselves to death for some worthless perfection that no one ever reaches – and even if you did, what fun would it be? I have found equal resonance with laid-back "trophy wives" and ambitious entrepreneurs. I want to be both. I want to be adored and a full version of myself for me and my loved ones. I want to have time for self-care, reading, learning, and goofing off with my kids. At the same time, I also desperately want to build something for myself and worth leaving to my girls. I want my own money to save and spend. I want to be taken seriously as someone who created something of value. This is where I jokingly decided that I would start telling people I was an "entrepreneurial trophy wife" just to get a laugh. Well, that's my origin story so far. Who knows where it'll go next? Since I'm now pushing 40, I feel like I have a few tricks I've learned along the way and enough grey hair (under the bleach) to pass out some sage wisdom, so here you go.

2

How to be a mom and a person all at the same time

I know not everyone wants to have kids, but if there's one thing I've learned from befriending and working with women of many walks of life, it's that if it's not kids, it's always something. Now, I know there are plenty of women out there who have managed to escape all family or social responsibility, and they are their own powerful little islands where they can just focus on self-care, careers, and pursuits without needing to give endlessly of themselves to others. I'm guessing that none of those women picked up this book. Most of the rest of us have children, aging parents or grandparents, and pursuits that bring us people who need our help. The list goes on. I'm not out here trying to only write from the mom perspective, but that's my perspective, so that's what you get. Children or life events may shake us up, whether we like it or not, but they also force us to grow.

I had already mentioned that I was hell-bent and determined not to change too much when I had kids. I thought I really liked the person I was and the life that I had, so I was going to fight to keep it. Of course, now it's easy for me to sit here and type that if I had only known the growth and happiness, as well as cash flow and self-esteem, that was waiting for me. Looking back, I see how limited my vision of happiness and myself was. You have to learn to see when you've outgrown your current avatar. While I don't feel very different from the person I was when I was younger, there are moments in my life where it feels as though I've lived through several versions of myself. While I used to think that perhaps this was a sign of my breaking sanity, I now feel like this is a superpower that has helped me immensely.

So let this be an introduction to persona jumping.

Recognize that there is a huge shift coming your way (like having a kid, becoming a care taker, loosing a job or even marrying your favorite person.)

Fully sit with the idea that there is a need to change.

You have to sort of accept this before you can jump off the cliff.

Take inventory of what traits you may need to be your happiest self in this new life. Think of what to keep and what go get. Try to not be too practical about this or you'll talk your self out of it.

Come up with who this new you is. What is her schedule, what are her values? Does she need to now slow down and enjoy that newborn stage? Does she need to buy some cute athletic sets and get out there and find her mojo? I would get out the notes on your phone and write that shit down. I never did at first and then I would always forget what I was supposed to be doing or being.

Start small but really once you decide you have to basically brainwash yourself into being this new you and then everything really does fall in line. Just start pick one thing and just do it.

Helpful ways to do this.

Think of someone real or even a character you read or saw in a movie.

Make a private Pinterest mood board.

Make a playlist that makes you feel the correct vibes.

Play out the way you want to live in your head and then just kind of throw yourself into it.

A good ole fashion makeover. I love a new haircut

and cleaning out my closet.

I know it may sound shallow, but the whole concept of dressing and presenting yourself for the life you want, not the one you have, is really true. After I had my first daughter, I remember pushing her around in the mall and catching a glimpse of my own reflection in an old shirt with holes and stains from my pregnancy. I had refused to get anything I liked better because I felt, as a new mom, that it was selfish of me. That's what I told myself. Looking back, I now realize that this feeling was motivated by my own insecurities and dissatisfaction with my body. I felt the need to starve and punish it until it looked the way I wanted it to again. However, I want to emphasize that you will never have that exact same body again. You may end up looking even better and being more fit than ever before, but it will not be in the same body or with the same self. You will have grown into an entirely new person, so it would be silly to think that you can squeeze your new self back into your old persona. This is why it is imperative to consciously choose a new self and actively work towards becoming that person. You have to eliminate all other options and commit to your decision. Once you set a standard for who you are and how you want to be treated and seen, then you can move forward.

I used to think that if I could just change my environment or circumstances, then I could finally transform into who I wanted to be. But now I realize that it's completely backwards. I have come to understand that you have to change yourself first, and then your life will change accordingly. I wish I could go back in time and tell my 15-year-old self this valuable lesson. Instead, I kept thinking that if I were in a different body, a different town, or a different family, my life would magically change. But the truth is, all I needed to do was change myself. I would have saved myself a lot of pain and heartache. This realization has been the hardest thing for me to grasp. I can't change anyone else. We are all responsible for our own journey in life, and we can't make excuses when it comes to becoming who we truly want to be.

In hindsight, having my entire persona destroyed by having kids was actually a good thing for me. It forced me out of the type of jobs I thought I wanted. Growing up, I had never been exceptional in school, sports, or social politics, so like many others, I endlessly pursued validation through my career, achievements, and degrees. I thought money sounded great, but having never had it, I didn't know what I was missing. However, I had always been surrounded by high achievers in the academic world, and I desperately wanted to succeed and be recognized for something I genuinely cared about. While I did experience some success in the fine arts field after college, I never pursued it in the traditional gallery sense due to the 2008 market crash and subsequently moving across the country with my now-husband in search of new adventures. This brought me to a scientific community in Eastern WA, where I worked a series of odd part-time jobs and a long stint in legal telecommunications working from home. Needless to say, none of these things brought me any meaning, desire, or a sense of exceptionality.

However, I was content and happy. I had love, health, we built a nice home, and embarked on as many adventures as we could afford. I convinced myself that it was fine to be unexceptional and simply be happy. There is so much to be said for reaching this point in life. Now, I realize that many people dream of and never achieve this level of contentment. I could almost write an entire prequel to this book on the joys of enjoying and being grateful for a simple life. So, I'm not here to deceive you and claim that you can hustle up a business while having a newborn or preschooler. In fact, I'm here to tell you the opposite.

If you can afford to live off just one income, even if it means using coupons for diapers and baby food, you should seriously consider taking a moment to relax. I believe that this "girl boss" and constant hustle culture that has affected millennial moms can be quite damaging. Personally, I spent a good amount of time knitting hats and watching marathons of "Ancient Aliens" on the History Channel with a baby asleep on me. As a mom of young children, I encourage you to take the time to daydream. What does your ideal situation look like? What big, wild dreams do you have? And what smaller steps can you take towards achieving them?

In my own experience, I initially thought I could sell a few knitted items on Etsy or in local eclectic shops. My goal was to make an extra $100 a month, as I was already spending a lot of time knitting. I figured that amount could be saved for vacations or shopping money. If it hadn't been for having children and being forced to reconsider the type of life I wanted, I might still be working for others doing things that are far below my creative capacity. Over time, my goals evolved as I had my second child, learned to spin yarn, and moved across the country. Although these events may seem random, the time I gave myself to daydream made them all fit together.

Having small children can disrupt your schedule and flow, as any new parent would agree. During my second pregnancy, when I was often sick and miserable, I spent a lot of sleepless nights teaching myself how to work a spinning wheel while watching Wes Anderson films and yearning to create something meaningful. Despite not being skilled in traditional artistic mediums such as drawing or painting, I found solace in the fiber arts world. The movement, flow, colors, textures, and artistic vision captivated me. So, I crafted a new vision for myself. I would not only make hand-knit items, but also create the yarn itself. I believed this would make my creations extra special and one-of-a-kind. All of this was happening during a chaotic period with a cross-country move, a 2 and 4-year-old, a stressed-out husband, a frazzled parrot, and a perfect dog. It was an incredibly challenging and overwhelming time, where I felt like my needs, body, and sanity were constantly pushed aside. Yet, I clung to the idea of creating something online, like a life raft.

To this day, whenever I come across a mom of young children trying to pursue anything, whether it's painting, selling Tupperware, or dog walking, I am always there to support her. You never know when that "silly" idea might be the one thing keeping that mom from feeling overwhelmed or reaching her breaking point.

Life always keeps moving, and during that time, I developed a supportive group of mom friends from our local church. They became my much-needed support system, especially when I felt like my husband was rarely around, and even when he was, he was preoccupied with his own stress and challenges. As our girls grew older and started preschool, things began to settle down, and we had the opportunity to go on a few vacations and catch our breath in the rhythm of everyday life.

During this period, I started delving into the world of online marketing and sales. It amazed me how much things had changed in such a short time. Now, it's possible to run a business selling homemade goods and services entirely online, without relying on marketplaces like Etsy or eBay. I strongly encourage you to create your own website or landing page as soon as possible. While there aren't many rules when it comes to building a personal brand, the quicker you establish an online presence and build an email list of people interested in hearing from you, the better.

I spent several years learning about online marketing and building my own business. It was exciting to see the potential income I could generate as an artist without any formal training in these new skills. I experimented with different methods, and while some were more successful than others, they all contributed to my growth in some way.

As I write this, it has been seven years since we moved and I started actively building my own business, not just relying on Etsy and hoping to crack the sales algorithm. Although I still feel like I have a long way to go and continually strive to keep up with the "big companies" in my industry, I have already achieved a level of growth and income that I couldn't have imagined when I first began. Working for myself, I can honestly say that I've made more money than I ever did when employed by someone else.

But beyond the financial aspect, the most significant achievement for me is that I have never once since moving here felt like I only had the roles of "Mom" and "Wife" in the world. While those roles are immensely important to me, it also feels right to add entrepreneur, writer, content creator, marketing director, and business owner to that list. It's challenging to put into words, but it's a feeling of everything falling into place, aligning with what I was always meant to do. I cherish having the time and freedom to prioritize my family, knowing that in doing so, I am also prioritizing myself.

As women, I strongly believe that the more we invest in ourselves and become obsessed with our own lives, the better we can uplift everyone in our immediate circle. Giving myself time and space allows me to have more to give to others, enabling me to be fully present with my kids and husband. Some might consider it self-centered, but I genuinely believe that as the woman in a household, we hold much power in either making or breaking it.

That's why I find it amusing when people dismissively say, "Oh, I'm just a stay-at-home mom" or "I only work part-time doing something insignificant, pretty much a housewife." I mean sure if you're laying around hating yourself and waiting on the world to validate you and make you feel seen and important you'll be waiting forever. If you're always pessimistic and easily upset then that's just going to come out as nit picking and micromanaging everyone in your life slowly driving them and you nuts. Unfortunately, I see many women my age falling into this pattern. I believe it stems from a need to feel important and in control, leading to becoming fixated on insignificant things like how to load the dishwasher or put away shoes.

When you're content with yourself and your overall life, it becomes much easier to let things slide. For me, considering the numerous responsibilities I already have of running multiple brands, overseeing marketing and sales, I don't want to be in charge of too much else.

In summary, life keeps moving, and during my journey, I discovered the importance of a supportive community, embraced the opportunities in online marketing, and achieved personal and professional growth. As women, empowering ourselves ultimately enriches the lives of those around us. Letting go of perfectionism and focusing on what truly matters brings fulfillment and allows us to thrive in multiple roles.

If my kids are trying to sweep and they miss a spot or don't hold the broom the way I would I really don't care. Same for my husband, I see that he's stressed and honestly we all need to be our own people he's not responsible for my 24/7 happiness and fulfillment anymore than I am of his. If you can manage your own energy, happiness and expectations even if all you get done all day is laundry and loading the dishwasher you'll notice a huge difference in everyone you live with and ultimately your own life. The only way I've found to do that is to really figure out who you want to be and then start walking it out as best you can. You have to have faith that it'll work out. Once you've done this work on clearing out your own hurts and demons you'll be able to bounce back so much faster from life's disappointments. This is why I think it's imperative that you become a mom and a person at the same time!

One of the main problems, I think most people run into is that they tell themselves the same stories over and over again. These stories may have been inspired by childhood or school. I think many of us grew up being sold this narrative that you had to either fully commit to being at home or having a high-powered career. You could choose to either be independent and the "breadwinner" or you were destined to just be dependent and second rate. Another common story is that people that came for money could have money, Only people with impressive college degree could be business owners, or successful, etc. For me, this problem mainly manifested in my beliefs about having extra money that I myself created as well as hang ups with my physical appearance. Most people may not agree that those hang-ups are related but for me those two things were definitely intertwined. I am a huge advocate for the "if you look better, you feel better and you will achieve more mentality."Feeling poorly about my body and then believing for years that there just wasn't anything I could do about it was really a problem that went hand in hand with feeling like academic achievement and success were all things that just were not in the cards for me. To me it seemed like it was just some genetic destiny, always putting me coming at the world from a place of always feeling defective. I eventually started noticing a reoccurring theme with everything I was listening to or reading, random podcast all the way to Bible verses. The general theme was anytime you ran into anything that was really giving you a major hang-up, stop and look at it and ask yourself or pray "is this really accurate?" I feel like most of the time the answer has always come back that it's not necessarily accurate or true. Especially if you take whatever the concern is and hold it up next to the founding tenants of your life or spiritual beliefs about yourself and how the world works and how God sees you.

Once you've pointed out to yourself that it's not necessarily written in stone and 100% true you can start coming up with a story that could be more true. An explantation that still seems believable but that pivots you and puts you in a direction where you can get out or around the problem instead of just being stuck forever believing "that's just how it is". You can apply the same tactic to so many topics. Ranging from "Everyone in my family struggles with weight gain and body image so I guess I have to be on a constant diet too." Or, "My family always lived barely paycheck to paycheck so I guess that's what we're going to have to do."

One of the all-time stupid stories that always played through my head for years was that I "wasn't the one of those girls" which now I'm not even sure what that even means, but it was definitely an idea I picked up along the way, growing up that somehow, my looks , family or personality meant that I was never going to be "that girl" somehow this stupid idea plagued so many parts of my life. Anytime something wasn't working out it would pop up and be like well. You're just not that girl that stuff works out for. Luckily, along the way, I also picked up this silly notion that I was a Smith(my maiden name) and Smith's had luck and that Smith luck always worked out (thanks dad). Also, My aunt on my mom's side of the family told awkward preteen me not to worry that women in our family never had trouble getting marriage proposals. I laughed about that tremendously at the time but it's funny how things stick with you as it turns out both sides of my family were right I definitely have never had trouble being lucky or getting marriage proposals.

Those are two obviously silly examples but when you're having some sort of depressive funk, sometimes thinking about something super silly and irrelevant but that somehow has run through in your life can be helpful. All you really have to do is find a different better way to look at whatever it is you're dealing with and then you can make what would be a problem into the reason that you're going to be successful just to spite the world.

I was just talking to a friend of mine today about how I feel like you could take my early 20s and pull it straight out of the timeline of my life and then I would look much more coherent. I feel like the person that I am now feels much more authentic to the person I started out as as a teenager. I feel like during and after college I tried really hard to be the type of person that I thought I was supposed to be to achieve the goals that I wanted. It kind of felt like wearing a costume the whole time.

We were talking about her daughter who's older than mine getting ready to figure out what type of college or curriculum she wanted to pursue how hard it can be at 17 or 18 to figure out what path you need to be on and what person you need to be working towards. I really wish I had more answers or solutions for people that age but it really seems like something that you just have to kind of live and figure out and hopefully not set yourself too far back along the way. The main thing that stands out to me is not over complicating things. I think it's easy to think that you have to go on this great journey of becoming a grown-up, but it might really be much more simple. I think you need to try to figure out what type of life would make you happy and then try to build a routine that is self sustaining and easy to build on. When I was a teenager, I wanted to own kind of a local arts venue. A very large part of my current work is artist promotion. It's honestly a big reason I'm writing this book. The two cornerstones of my life seem to be supporting a secure, happy family unit and encouraging people who have art, thoughts, and ideas that need to get into the world.

My point is, as a woman, you have to listen to that voice in your heart and pick a direction you feel pulled towards. But there is also a good bit of just letting go and taking the leap. You're not going to get it right the first time, but in my experience, as long as you keep checking in with that tug in your gut and get to know yourself well enough to distinguish that true voice from the voice of the world and all its distractions and dead ends, you'll eventually end up where you need to be.

Once you've pointed out to yourself that it's not necessarily written in stone and 100% true you can start coming up with a story that could be more true. An explantation that still seems believable but that pivots you and puts you in a direction where you can get out or around the problem instead of just being stuck forever believing "that's just how it is". You can apply the same tactic to so many topics. Ranging from "Everyone in my family struggles with weight gain and body image so I guess I have to be on a constant diet too." Or, "My family always lived barely paycheck to paycheck so I guess that's what we're going to have to do."

3

You can be more than one thing at a time

For years I always felt like when I reached some new level of success I would feel or look different or more powerful. I always felt like I was stuck in the poor post-college job hunt identity or the new mom identity. If I could just reach the level of success where people would recognize me as a "successful business owner," then my grooming and outlook would naturally improve.

I don't know why it has taken me so long to figure out that most successful people probably don't even feel particularly successful themselves. We all contain contradictions, living at once in messy and successful parts of our lives. I've finally figured out that it's not just the level of success you have that matters, but how you hold yourself in relation to others. The most successful people I know are the ones who have figured out how to be both messy and together. They have learned to be content with themselves in ways that don't depend on external validation, or at least not too much. They have learned to hold the tension between the two sides of their lives, and they do not feel that one needs to be sacrificed for the other. They are working on themselves every day, even if they aren't always aware of it. They know that they can't be perfect but they can always be better. You never reach a point where someone comes in with a gold star and tells you that you made it. If you had told me when I first began selling hats on Etsy that one day my yarns and spinning fiber would be included at a booth at Vogue Knitting Live, I would have said that would be the validation I needed to feel like I'd made it. While I am incredibly proud that this happened I also have a list in my head to disqualify why it wasn't as important as it sounded. This is what we all do. I read somewhere one time that the version of ourselves that we know to be ourselves doesn't exist to anyone else. My head hasn't stopped hurting thinking about this yet. It's kind of liberating too. All of the imperfections and hang-ups that the you in your head is so painfully aware of only really exist there. So using my Vogue knitting example,

36

in my head I have all of these reasons why this wasn't as much of a milestone as it could be. To a different version of me just starting out this would have been an ultimate moment of having arrived. Having become a bit "known online" even if it wasn't initially, what I set out to do has forced me to accept that the version of me, that people see, and experience online is not necessarily the real me. Not that I'm trying to be misleading, but rather that there is no way for anyone to interpret me the way I do. I figured could either be really stressed out about this , running around trying to make sure I was being perceived correctly or I could use this alter ego to my advantage. I slowly started to just project the person I wanted to be seen as instead of worrying about being "a poser". What I'm trying to say is if we're all being somewhat delusional anyway you might as well use that as a power for good instead of a stumbling block of imposter syndrome.

If you want to be a business owner you need to treat it that way. Open a separate checking account, file the appropriate paperwork and keep track of tax write-offs.

TELL PEOPLE YOU ARE A BUSINESS OWNER or whatever your thing is. I struggled with this FOREVER. I would trip over my words anytime someone would ask. It usually landed between stay-at-home mom and " I have a yarn thing…"

If you want to be adored by your family act like you adore yourself and expect it. It might throw you off for a minute but you will start seeing yourself as worthy of being cared for. You don't have to be the worn-out milk cow at the end of the day. Learn to say No and have it not be a big deal.

If you want to feel hot or pretty etc. Start doing that right now! Right this damn minute. Especially if you're a mom of little children. I wish I had a redo on the 3-5 years I walked around in dirty maternity clothes because I had lost my body and identity. As a result, I never felt any better. We can't all afford to do all the things but grab some toe nail polish and a box of washout toner for your hair if you need to but it'll make you feel so much better. Find some people , celebrities, influencers or someone you admire and just copy them till you get inspired. Be patient with yourself and don't expect yourself to be perfect. It takes time to find yourself again but it will happen. You don't have to go out and buy a new wardrobe right away just take a few steps towards the you, you'd like to be. It's not about being perfect but it's about feeling good in your own skin. I know how hard it is to get out of bed and face the world when you don't feel like yourself. I think picking an actionable "inspiration person" is important. For instance, Im petite build and curvy it used be very hard to find clothes that I liked and

I always just felt short and thick in comparison to everyone. This was just made worse if I was looking at petite but slim ladies like Reese Witherspoon, or tall glamorous ladies like most models. I also found that what worked for many moms where I lived (loose tunic tops and leggings) made me look like a potato.

Once I discovered some influencers on social media who looked like me it became so much easier to shop and feel good about my own body. The same strategy can be used for makeup and hair. Don't try to be something you're not.

Figure out who you want to be and then start making the most basic steps towards holding yourself accountable. We all have a loud internal voice or critic so if you can start impressing your internal monologue it'll start becoming your friend and not your enemy. It's amazing the silly beliefs we can pick up along the way even from well-meaning loved ones when we're young. I have had to try so hard to un-program my own brain. I had spent years believing " I just wasn't one of those girls " I don't even know what that means! Since I like practical steps that I can highlight in books here you go.

Figure out what personas you'd like to take on more in your life. Even if it seems silly. Here are a few. Business owner, Wealthy, Rested, Athletic , Hot, Sexy, Well Read, Runner , Yogi, Writer, Fun Mom,

Adventurer

Think about all the reasons that your inner critic says you can't do or be those things. (this part is always super easy for me. Write them down so you can be specific about it.

Go through your list of reasons that your inner critic just pointed out an then write down what you think the woman who would embody those things would do or be instead. Ex. I want to be an adventurer who's hot and athletic and kind of cool and sexy (what can I say I grew up playing tomb raider and I have an Anthropology. degree) My brain of course points out that I'm a 30 something Mom who isn't Angelia Jolie and I can't jump off a curb without twisting my ankle... If I stop beating myself up I can look at this and see what the brass tacks of my fantasy are. I would like to feel healthy, strong, smart, driven, and engaged in something I find interesting or engaging. Tan, fitter, flexible, sexy, maybe look cute in some solid color tank tops and boots..Do more things outside like hiking or ropes courses or a fun vacation with sightseeing.

See that those descriptions are probably more attainable and then write down even the dumbest sounding things that might get you more in that vibe. Ex. Throw out frumpy stained ripped-up clothing that I hate. Listen to a different Pandora station, and find some Podcast that engages you.

Get some new books, blog something, get a new hobby. Start working out or doing what you can to feel more athletic. Start out doing planks or push-ups or something where you can count and see that you are getting a bit better. Buy some solid-color tank tops and boots to go on walks vs the "Mom Life" t-shirts or whatever non-sexy bullshit you felt pressured into wearing by society.

Just keep making those small changes for at least 1-3 months and then you'll really start to prove to your inner critic that hey you are sticking to it and feeling different and maybe you are that type of girl after all... It'll start to snowball I promise.

So this is the part where you accuse me of trying to make you brainwash yourself. Well, you're exactly right. I spent most of my life trying to outsmart everything. Learning disabilities, P.E class, grades, College applications, jobs that were so boring or stressful I wanted to die, feeling poor, feeling unworthy, feeling weird and uncool and not liked or understood. I was always convinced that if I was charming enough or tried hard enough or saved enough maybe one day I could scrape by and have some small part of what I wanted. I of course never dared to think of having what I really wanted because " I wasn't one of those girls" whatever the fuck that meant. I was already brainwashed. I just didn't know it. I learned that so many of my assumptions about life and myself were wrong or at least could be improved.

I had grown up being told that the women in my family weren't good at sports, or math, being skinny, enjoying food without heaps of guilt, trying on clothes without feeling bad about how they looked on, etc. I thought that rich people were somehow bad, lucky or greedy and had probably sacrificed something good to have money.

It was always sort of seen as virtuous to be scraping by. It was this feeling of we're all in it together, we're all together in the lack and struggle. I realized that I was so brainwashed I didn't even realize that the reason I felt so awkward most of my life was I was living as the wrong person. I was playing the game as the wrong avatar. So I say go ahead, be delusional, if you feel uncomfortable around the people you're around try to move or get new friends. Once you start making some small changes to actually have things you enjoy in your life and your day you'll love how fast things can change. Once you start to win over that voice in your head and the two of you become friends worlds will shift and life will change you just have to trust me. Stop using being one thing as an excuse to not have things that you want. YOU CAN BE MORE THAN ONE THING! You don't have to wait to finish one phase of life to give yourself permission to live and be happy.

Examples:

I can't be a Mom and be successful at anything else. (You can be a Mom and in the time and capacity that you have you can find something for yourself that can grow as your children get older)

I can't be broke and feel abundant (start being grateful for literally everything including breathing and your loved ones being healthy)

I can't be in the body I have and feel attractive(purge stuff you hate, Look at body type profiles and color charts get help from something like stitch fix)

The person that I am now feels much more authentic to the person I started out as a teenager. I have found that it's much easier for me to try not to get too deep into a funk than to try to pull myself out afterward. This is admittedly not always easy when something frustrating happens. I try not to make it really mean anything about me or my life. I try to just see it as something that happened and something that will pass. This works much better for smaller frustrations and inconveniences and not major life-altering tragedies that's not what I'm talking about here. I'm definitely not trying to belittle any actual pain and suffering in your life. Comedian Lewis CK has a great bit about how

43

magical it is to be flying in an airplane. The journey that people used to die on trying to go from one side of the country to the other is now something you can easily enjoy while listening to a podcast. I always stop and listen to this joke whenever I hear him tell it because I get tremendously stressed out about airports. The idea of giving away all of your choices to people who manage airlines, and that your schedule can get easily thrown off completely unnerves me. His words are a great reminder that what seems like a major catastrophe to me is actually part of something that's pretty amazing and convenient compared to life in general for many people across the world. Don't get me wrong. I'm still a complete psycho when it comes to going to the airport but at least I'm trying my best to not catastrophize the situation every time something seems like it might be falling apart. So try your best to hold onto the vision of the life you want and the person you want to be and let the bullshit go. In your head just imagine that all of the little inconveniences and setbacks are so completely unrelated to you that they will quickly fall away.

4

"feminine" is the new F word

The older I've gotten the more I've realized that if something feels good or exciting to you then as long as it's healthy and within reason, there's probably a nugget of something there that your soul really longs for. I was raised by a Forester and a Green House Manager so let's just say it wasn't the "girliest" of upbringings. As I remember the words, girly, cheerleader, pretty much anything pink or blonde or over the top was looked down on. As far as I could tell being a woman meant being a no-fuss all-natural hippy type or the campy 1950's pin-up girl art my Dad collected. It took me most of my adult life well past having kids to really embrace that I'm actually really girly. Despite my dirty sense of humor, love of dive bars, punk bands, and natural yearning for adventure I'm actually very feminine. That felt dirty even typing that… However, learning to embrace being the type of person that felt best to me has really made a big difference in my happiness. Now I'm not saying what appeals to me has to appeal to everyone I'm just saying when I stopped turning my nose up at the secret forbidden fruit of femininity I actually felt much more powerful and comfortable in my own skin. This has also worked well with my business and personal branding. Even in the fiber arts world, I have felt pressure to conform to a certain image, either too wholesome or too crunchy to feel comfortable. My website like my wardrobe has run the gamut between trying to fit the more modest yet pretty womanly "mom vibe" to the "look how polished and professional I am" clean retail website look. I have had the worst time marring the different parts of myself and my brand together. I finally had to decide that I may not be everyone's cup of tea, people may look at me or my work and judge me for being silly, vapid, trashy, or just plain awkward in their eyes. I'm ok with it. For me focusing on being the woman I want to be instead of trying to force myself into some sort of career woman in a man's world persona to be taken seriously has made life so much easier. I've been taking the time to focus on what makes me happy, what I want my life to look like, and how I can make that happen. I'm learning how to take care of myself and let go of things that don't serve me. It's a process but one that is worth it! I know everyone's vibe is going to be different so please forgive me for generalizing but I'm assuming if you've gotten this far in this book we're probably somewhat similar. Here are some points that have helped me embrace my inner feminine.

Work on the schedule and flow that fits your life. Stop trying to make it match a 9-5. Right now I'm writing this after cleaning up dinner with my kids and before we finish this Taylor Swift documentary they are excited about. In my mind, I still fantasize about having this nice established work time where I sit down, crunch numbers, and have deep thoughts but things were never happening waiting for that perfect scenario. Now I'm getting bookkeeping, writing, editing, and marketing done in 30-minute windows throughout the day anywhere from 5 am- to midnight depending. I personally think by nature women are the flow. We are in tune with our environments, family, and the general energy around us. Being able to ebb and flow as needed especially if you have young children is important.

Wear what you want, If you work at home or in your own office wear what you want! I know I have fully embraced the cute luxe Athleisure lifestyle. I need something I can drop the kids off in, do a quick workout, write, film, pick up groceries, and maybe grab a coffee in. I used to be one of those people that felt like I was either "dressed" or not. When my first daughter was born I didn't own a single pair of leggings! Finding that middle ground has made my life so much more streamlined. Figure out what that is for you. I'm sure people think I look funny in band tees and form-fitting leggings or a slinky cotton dress but that's my idea of attractive daily wear.

Lean back some and let other people help you and learn to receive. This one can be so hard, I don't know why we all think we have to prove our worth to ourselves and the world but holding up this list of all of the things we accomplished with no help. I'll touch on this in a whole chapter later. I think stopping to breathe and enjoy life is key.

Be nice to yourself! We've all heard this a million times but if you always put yourself last you'll be less effective, giving, and happy. I have two daughters, what am I giving them to look forward to growing up if I make it look miserable? I don't want them to think all they do is grow up and then get ignored by everyone. You can't martyr your way into people loving you. I have probably the best family ever and not once have any of them stopped and been like "Wow, Mom is just killing it putting all of us first. She's so amazing let's all give her compliments

48

and foot rubs!" We all know them, those peers who are always on Facebook crying about how hard and unfair life is asking for prayers (but not asking for help or guidance just sympathy and attention). I'm no stranger to life being hard. I could give you a long list of ways life has been hard for me but I'm grounded enough to know that the world is full of people who would trade anything for my problems. I'm just saying if you need help, ask for some(see my previous point) say THANK YOU, and then savor that feeling of being loved and cared for by the universe even if it was just letting the bag boy at the store help you instead of fighting with all the bags yourself, dropping your keys and then getting your cortisol all out of wack.

To me, my family seems to work better when we're all doing a good job of what our tasks are and staying in our own lane versus trying to do everything 50/50. This of course is going to look different for every family group but finding some things to " let go of" instead of wearing yourself out and fussing at everyone for not doing things the way you think they should be done. Most recently it occurred to me that the last 30 minutes or so before bedtime for the kids was getting on my nerves. By that point, I was worn out from the day and not in the best of moods. I wear down in the evening and was becoming really angry and resentful that bedtime always seemed to involve the girls getting super hyped up or argumentative about stupid stuff and then I'd end up dragging them both to bed in a bad mood and then feeling like a terrible mom right at the end of the day even though everything else that day had gone great. So I asked my husband if he could be in charge of bedtime instead of me assuming it was a normal night and he was home. This let me hug everyone and tell them I loved them and good night and let him have the last 15 minutes to tuck everyone in. Now this doesn't go perfectly every night but it has really made my night go better and he didn't seem to mind at all. To him, it's no big deal but to me, it really took a frustrating load off the end of my night. The girls listen to him better than me at the end of the day and it lets me go unwind and take a shower in peace. I bet there are silly little pressure points in your life that someone can help with and that free you up to be a better you for the people in your life.

5

Only boring people are board - why the world needs more weirdos

I have concluded that I'm not cut out to be normal, better yet I actively try to avoid boring people at all costs. This works out pretty great for me because I have meticulously arranged my life to only have to spend any amount of effort on people who are also cool. Now this lifestyle has taken me years to cultivate and it's not for the easily lonely or faint of heart. Sometimes I forget how good I've gotten at this until I'm forced to mingle with the masses. There is absolutely nothing better than finding other people who are also weird as shit and then making wonderful friendships. Thanks to the internet you can even have these friendships long distance. I love knowing that as I'm sitting up way too late after my family has gone to sleep, typing away listening to

Koe Wetzel, surrounded by rocks my kids brought home and yarn that's going out tomorrow in the mail that my friend in South Knoxville is also awake online, wearing a vintage house dress and living in her " hippy shack" as she calls it. It's great to be an outlier. You can either let life happen to you or you can happen to life. I think as women we should embrace being " a lot" or "too much". It sucks because the older you get the more side eye you acquire if you don't walk the line. I don't want to fit comfortably into anyone's little place for me. I want to be fun and big and take up space. Even if you are working a more typical 9-5 you can still let your nerdy obsessions loose in your spare time. Get super passionate about sourdough or brisket. Make the best damn potato salad the world has ever known. Watch all of the extended LOTRings movies while eating hummus and knitting, Be the most swifty-est of Taylor Swift fans just don't be boring!

Learn to talk less, you don't have to fill all the voids and silent times. When you talk have something cool to add, a good joke or stupid story. Kids are great at this. They can tell you everything you never knew you needed to know about lima beans or something equally random but it's still fantastic.

It doesn't matter if you ever monetize this or not. Just make sure to really dig into your weirdness. However, if you have the entrepreneurial bug like

I do it'll become the ultimate inch to scratch if you play your cards right. There are an endless amount of options on how to turn something you love into a way to reach others or make some cash. The two really don't even have to be connected. If your passion is buying all of the purses that make you happy or having the most decked-out front porch in suburbia it's cool to get some extra cash from a side hustle. It can be something nuts like selling yarn like me to online freelance work like medical record coding or copywriting. There are so many ways to fund what you love. My friend with the cool "Hippy Shack" I mentioned is a stay-at-home mom who has transformed into the niche boutique Airbnb queen of the Knox area. She's out there decorating houses with weird shit and getting paid for it. She's one of my local heroes for sure.

While you don't have to "be your own brand" it is helpful to be true to yourself. I have to say I really fought this for years. I wanted my company to be its own thing separate from my personality and style. I went through several website makeovers in the course of a few years. I tried making it slick and artsy, I tried communal, crunchy, and welcoming. I even tried to copy the layout of popular e-commerce sites. For me at least what has felt the most authentic was to accept that I needed to be the figurehead of my business. After years of resisting, I decided to let my freak flag fly a bit when it came to my business. This may seem more natural to you as well if you like myself fall into more of a teaching or lifestyle category. If you are selling things on an Amazon storefront or more of a system-based web service then you can probably get away with having a friendly brand that's just clean and professional without the need to really be involved yourself if you want but I would argue that even with those sorts of businesses the most memorial ones are the ones where you really feel like you know and life something about the business. Like it or not the influencer society is upon us. Social media has made even already famous people and brands have to scramble to develop some sort of likability or relatability online. Even if they are playing the villain having a memorial avatar of sorts helps them to become sought after online. Everyone I have talked to from small business owners, real estate agents, and writers, all of us struggle with imposter syndrome. That feeling of who am I to stand out or be important. How could anyone care what I have to say on any given topic? If I'm being honest this is the chorus in my head I'm having to fight right now as I write this book. However, I do believe in following all of those hunches and feelings from the great beyond so here I am. I have a lot to say as it turns out and half the time the only one in my real life listening is my dog. However, I have enough friends in real life and mostly online who seem to appreciate my point of view and accomplishments so far so it's my job to get out of my own way and keep talking and posting and writing because it may help someone somewhere that I'll never know. The world is becoming more and more disconnected and while I know the Internet gets a lot of blame here I also know that I for one would have a much lonelier life without the voices, faces, mentors, teachers, and friends I have found online. They say that the people you become most like are the 5 people you spend the most time with and for me on a regular basis, a decent chunk of that influence is coming from artists, writers, and creators online. If you grow up in a small town or place where your dreams and goals never fit in you may need to look a bit further out. Likewise, if you are a stay-at-home care taker etc where you feel isolated in the point of life that you're in. You can't look for your partner if you have one to fill all of the holes in your life. This is where being true to yourself and your work comes in (I promise I normally bring things full circle eventually) No matter what your passion project is if you give people a sense of friendliness and camaraderie they will be more interested in what you offering not to mention you may have a greater impact on making them feel less alone. That's my prediction anyway. I think that as we go forward the people who encourage and connect with the most hearts will come out ahead. I think we're all more lonely than we know and human connection is important. So while I know I'm to for everyone I do know that my less-than-perfect somewhat off self, has made some people feel less alone. Being a misfit in public lets others feel like they have a place to fit in.

One thing I have to say I like about getting older is that you just stop giving a shit. At this rate, by the time I'm an old lady, I'm going to be hard to handle. It makes me sad to think about how large of a chunk of my life I spent playing it safe in one way or another trying to be nice and agreeable. Growing up always sticking out for all the wrong reasons there is a great appeal to fitting in with your peers and being deemed just right and desired. I have to say one of my least favorite experiences was job interviews. I knew I was charming, I knew I was good at talking and being engaging but I hated the idea of having to sell someone not just on me as a person but as me for the right fit for their little square box they were looking to fill. I could sell you on me, however, I was never as good at selling people on the idea that I was a good fit for their career type job. I would always come away feeling super dejected. While it is scary to put yourself out there with starting your own business or becoming a content creator of some sort at least you know that you are standing on firm ground with your own two feet. Find out what is the most authentic version of you. Even if it's not cool. Style comes and goes all the time. I love a good trend but you have to learn to take what feels good to you and let the rest go. Keep what is you and stand on it. Be nerdy, hot, athletic, or laid back. Stand on it.

6

Resolve to get kicked out of some groups

It's late and I'm not sure if this is a life tip or a business tip but here you go. I spent most of my "business life" trying to not ruffle too many feathers and play by the rules. Now I know you're like Erin you own a business that sells yarn how many rules can there be? Well, I would have to agree with you except the fiber arts world like any other world has its cliques and expectations of conduct. I tried to not be salesy, not show cleavage or thighs in my videos, or say anything not PC and agreed upon by the collective narrative. Well, it sort of worked but it never felt right. After reading books and following other women on the internet who were just themselves in their niche I decided what the hell

I'll just be myself. Now I wish I could tell you that after making that shift the heavens opened up and everything just clicked. In some ways it did but in other ways (looking at you Instagram algorithm) not so much. However I feel so much happier now, things are so much easier now. The people who like my brand really like my brand for the right reasons. Selfish motives aside I feel like the people who have found me online also don't fit in. People often find it comforting to have someone who shares their interests and outlook I think that's why I wear my heart on my sleeve because people need to know what they're getting. They need to know that I'm not trying to push an agenda on them and that I'm being genuine for me that means being honest about who I am and what I want. However, I have had to grow a thicker skin when it comes to being direct and running my business from a place of not trying to please the masses.

I keep getting kicked out of Facebook fiber arts groups it's become almost a goal at this point. It normally goes something like this: Someone tags me in a post where someone is asking about something I know something about. I answer the question and try to be helpful like a dumb ass and then I get kicked out for " being salesy" I'm still not too sure how answering a question that you are asked about makes you the bad guy but welcome to the butthurtness of the internet. Instead of getting mad I now just screenshot it and laugh about it with my friends. I always get tons of feedback from other people who feel the same way. A marketer I admire talks about how you need to cultivate an "attractive character" for your business. The idea being that for ads and marketing purposes, you need a character or vibe that your target audience responds well to. This "attractive character" does not have to be you as the owner necessary but just sort of the voice of the brand. While this all makes sense to me and I don't disagree with it. For me, it all started to feel much more comfortable when I let my voice be the "brand voice."

I learned this firsthand with my work after a second brand that I had inherited " My Local Wool" started feeling awkward to me on Instagram. I was trying so hard to let this separate brand and business that I had taken over from the founder have its own vibe separate from me. I was trying to respect how it had started and the hopes and ideals of the project but I felt like I had accidentally taken away my authority to have a voice in the brand. When we started getting online trolls on that account it was finally the motivation that I needed to pretty much pull the plug on this separate website and brand and just take the good and combine it with my website " Crafty Housewife Yarns". I found that as soon as

I made this switch and added this to my voice and brand the more empowered I felt around making good business decisions. This hit home for me that, for me anyway, having the brand voice be my voice and listening to my intuition made all the difference. Here are some tips for finding and having your voice for your business or project.

Make a list of your favorite colors, fonts, and keywords. What do you respond to? For me, it was helpful to almost think of this like building a wardrobe. What feels good on you, I spent way too long trying to make myself and my work more polished or serious than I am as a person. This made it feel very unauthentic.

Think about what type of people you want to work with/for. Trust me if you start not jiving with your " ideal audience" the whole thing will feel forced.

When planning infrastructure look at what seems the easiest and most flowy to you. Making things complicated is not the answer. It may work for other people but if it's confusing to you, then you won't be able to get and stay behind it.

If you're going to stand for anything you're probably going to " trigger" some people. I feel like this used to be harder to do. I feel like so many people get bent out of shape, triggered, or disrespected (especially online) by basically everything. So if you're trying to just coast along and not annoy anyone you're going to fade into the great flood. The target for offense just keeps getting bigger and bigger so stepping on someone's feelings is unavoidable. I feel like this weeding out of "giving a shit about people's feelings" can be cathartic in both business and personal life. I was just on Facebook trying to catch up on what my friends were up to this weekend and there it is some random person having a statement about something I think is very eye-roll-inducing. I realized I had no clue why I was even seeing this person's content. They were literally the girlfriend of someone my husband worked with like 15 years ago. I never really jived with these people in real life, I don't need to see her bullshit. So I went through and "unfriended" a bunch of people that I realized they had reached out to me and I'd just been dragging along this relationship I never wanted in the first place. I didn't need their noise in my head, I didn't need them seeing my life that closely. It can be so easy, especially as women to feel like we have to be friendly with any mom from a playdate or the wife of your husband's friend. I've run into the same with branding and business. I went through about a 2-year stint where my website and brand was trying hard to be more crunchy and sweetsie than what I resonate with. It was from my fear and limiting belief that I would only be likable/make money and be successful if I fit the mold of what others liked. So as you see this is something I'm still learning and working on myself. One thing that has been undeniable for me is building a brand and business has forced me to hone my own beliefs and core values. Living life and working more in tune with my truth has been liberating for sure. It's like proving your bravery to yourself over and over again.

7

It's ok for things to be calm

I t's ok for things to be calm

This week has been the week after fall break for my kids so it's been this weird almost hung-over feeling after having a week of nonstop activities to oversee for my kids and all of their friends. So this week in comparison has seemed really quiet. Almost too quiet. I've had to fight the feelings of guilt or worry all week with that dreaded I'm not doing enough feeling. The truth is, it's ok to have quiet weeks. It's hard to not feel guilty or worried when things are calm and quiet. If you grew up used to lots of stress or the bottom dropping out from under you it can be a challenge to just accept that things can be stable and calm. I think I always had this feeling that I had to be on constant guard against something, keeping a watchful eye for anything that seemed like

64

it could be a red flag of emotional or financial ruin being just around the corner. I think the trick is to keep an eye out for red flags in the people and circumstances you let close to you while also trying to really relax into trusting God or the Universe or whatever it is you believe in. I really struggled with this and I eventually figured out that my hyper-vigilance and fixation on checking the "safeness" of every aspect of my life definitely flared up if I was feeling anxious. So this led me to believe that this was probably not a super accurate reflection of what was true but more some sort of crazy chemical, hormone or wiring in my own head. If that was the case then it wasn't too hard to start believing that I could believe that I was lucky and blessed and that things were always working out of me. When I started looking at it that way it seemed to me that I'd been through a lot of unstable shit and challenges that didn't seem fantastic at the time but that some force had always been there getting me out of any jam I was ever in. I had learned that the rules of school and success had never applied to me for good so they sure didn't have to apply to me for bad either. I had decided I was always the exception and not the rule and that things just worked of me even when it seemed rocky.

It can be so easy to get sucked into the narrative that you always have to be grinding it out in some way or you just weren't working hard enough and therefore not deserving in some way. It may work that way for some people but that hasn't proven true for me. It reminds me of the image on the tarot card "temperance", it's normally a woman pouring water back and forth between two cups. The idea is that you don't get balance by having everything even and equal, but rather by pouring your energy back and forth. Anyone with "ADHD" or similar wiring can tell you how it goes. You can go from procrastinating and doing what looks like nothing and then all of a sudden spring into action and get more done in an hour than most people did all afternoon. Sometimes you have to pour yourself fully into your family or self-care, other times you have to really get it in gear and start checking off boxes to move your work or project forward. I have tried and failed so many times to keep a nice little schedule with blocks of time for different activities. I have found rather that having a big-picture goal and some smaller goals to get there works best. Then you have to gauge where you're at and what will make your plan work best. Sometimes you do have to really hit a deadline and then you have to just hype yourself up and get really into being the person who would have that done and then become that. Sometimes you just have to trick yourself into being the person who gets the life you want.

Other times you have to really learn to go back and forth and not beat yourself up along the way. I think it's important to set goals and then break them down into smaller parts, but you also have to be flexible. You'll never get anything done if you're not ready to let go of your original plan and adjust along the way. Just remember as tempting as it can be to join the parade of people telling you how stressed, busy, and miserable they are sometimes it's good to just be happy. Enjoy what you're doing. Enjoy what you're building even if it's just in the little corners of the day in-between your day job you want to leave or never-ending loads of laundry. It's ok (and probably even good) to not feed into this constant narrative as women that we're only worth as much as we serve others and grind ourselves down. It's not just ok to be happy, it's also ok to be selfish. It's ok to put yourself first and make decisions that are good for you instead of always putting others first. I have two daughters I don't want them to grow up thinking the only way to win is to make themselves smaller and smaller. Of course, we all need to have great work ethics but it may be worth writing down all the things that you are doing right and letting that be good for a while. I've heard it often called "inspired action" in many sermons and books. I love it. The idea of really stopping long enough to pray or look inward and really feel into what is the next right thing and then just doing that. Ask what " has to " happen like the world will stop if you don't do it then after that everything else can be flexible. Instead of doing everything try to do the next right thing. Before you start complaining that you don't know what that is just stop and really think. I'm sure you do, you just need to give yourself and the Universe a little more credit for guidance. You know more than you think. It can be helpful to recognize within yourself if you're in a funk you need to break out of or if it's a problem you really need help to get out of.

If I can see that I'm getting stuck in my head and purposefully try to redirect my thoughts, actions, and energy it can really help me to stay calm and happy. This can be especially helpful if you start noticing that your fixation on problems stems more from a place of fear of things being calm than from real problems.

With practice, this will become more and more natural. You just have to see your fears for what they are. Pull them out one by one to examine them closer and this will quickly take some of the power out of them. We've all heard the advice just "write a new story" and while I admit this can seem trite there is a bit of magic in doing so. We so easily tell ourselves stories every day; how we messed up and we're dumb, fat and everyone thinks

68

we're embarrassing. How about instead tell yourself different stories? You probably won't overnight turn into believing you're amazing but how about you could start reframing one of those nagging scenarios that pops into your head at night. Try to see how something may not have worked out because you were being saved for something better down the line. I was devastated when I was unable to go on with grad school after college due to conflicts with required courses and my learning disabilities. However, I now know that I would have really struggled to keep the relationship with my boyfriend (now husband) together. My children could have never been born, I would have never loved working in the fine art market in Charleston or had any of the other wonderful things happen to me. So from here, it looks like what was a huge letdown and something I felt badly about myself was really a great blessing that has led to so many pivotal parts of my life. If you would like a more vain and down-to-earth example having big hips and a big butt was something I was incredibly self-conscious about all through my youth (it was the late 90's early 2000s) I never would have guessed that being curvier would end up being something I get many compliments about now that I'm older. It's taken me years to reframe the idea that "looking my best" didn't mean starvation and trying to look as small as possible.

I bet there are many things big and small past and present you can start to take apart. All you have to do is narrow down the actual thought versus just a nameless nagging feeling. After that just ask yourself what is a better, even slightly better way you could see that. You can literally inch your way out of it over time. Once you get that belief to neutral then you can start trying to build on positive feelings from there. Once you start believing the more positive stories about your life I promise you'll look around and you'll be a whole new person. It's like magic.

8

Boundaries and standards

A nytime I talk to a group of women for any amount of time at parties, church, moms groups, or in entrepreneur groups one thing quickly stands out as a problem, setting and keeping boundaries. While no one is perfect here I do think I struggle with this less than most. My biggest boundary pushers are my two young daughters who are just too much like their Mama. That could be a whole chapter by itself that I'm probably not qualified to write. For the most part, I think if you replace the word boundaries with standards it'll quickly help you to set and hold them. As women most of us really want to be seen as "nice" people I am luckily not so afflicted with this and I'm a bit of a bitch so I'm here to help you.

Saying yes to everything, to everyone, especially things that you know will drain you and are not necessary to kicking your own personal vision a little further down the road should be avoided at all costs. We all need to realize how much energy, love passion and life force we pour into everything and everyone. While we all like to think that we have a never-ending supply of energy we don't. Some of us get run down faster than others. You really have to get to know your own flow in this way. I for example know that I'm good to go in the morning, I need to crash and have some decompression/recharging time in the afternoon and then I can be nice and loving to people again for the rest of the day. This is why my current workflow looks something like this on an ideal day.

5 am wake up with my husband, go downstairs and work on a journal, bible study, good book, etc. This is when I drink coffee, think, pray on things, and try to get my head on straight. I will normally get on the computer around 6 and check emails, put out fires check bank accounts, website orders, staff workflow, etc.

7-7:45 ish get kids up and to school

8-around 1 I'll do whatever work/home/gym stuff needs to happen that day.

I have learned that after I eat I need a "brain break" to just kind of zone out and be useless before the kids get home. I used to feel bad about not using all of my kid's free time to the max but I have come to really value having some time to recharge my batteries before dealing with homework, dinner, all of the neighbor kids, and more work later in the day. Being "selfish" and giving myself some time to enjoy while everyone is out even if the laundry is sitting there and there is still work to be done really helps me to be the person that my family, friends, and customers deserve not the worn-out resentful crazy lady I would be otherwise. I have found that when I am able to relax, unwind, and take time for myself, it makes me more patient with my family. It also helps me foster better relationships with friends and customers because I am not the frazzled mom who can't remember what day it is anymore. Now believe me every day does not go this way, all sorts of things will throw this off track but this is what I shoot for. If you just make it a standard for what you need to feel your best instead of thinking it's some sort of mean boundary you're trying to uphold it seems easier. You can't do everything for everyone all the time. This works in the personal and work sphere. I can't always do all of the kid stuff at school, being a homeroom mom, PTA mom, etc is not my strong suit. I also know my kids don't really care so this is not a priority for me. My girls are much happier when we go walk around shops or get coffee together. My husband doesn't require someone to chase after him to feel loved, he'd much rather me be healthy and happy to hang out with him instead. As women, I think it's easy for us to fall into the trap of thinking that we have to be everything for everyone all the time or else we lose value, I've been experimenting with leaning back more, especially at home. my girls are getting older and they're able to do things for themselves so I don't have to be the one to do everything. That of course can be hard to do because as a mom you always feel like you're the one that can do everything best and that that somehow demonstrates love and affection to your family. In my experience, all these little ways that we think demonstrate our love to our families, they aren't even noticing, and then we slowly become resentful and angry.

With work, especially if you're going to work for yourself you have to learn to make some boundaries fast. When my business was just starting out it was much easier to check off all of the outstanding orders and then take a deep breath and feel on top of things. Now thanks to growth and being a subscription-based e-commerce business there are ALWAYS outstanding orders. This means that I had to be able to switch off " work" even if I wasn't "done". Being a business owner means that work is never really at a stopping point. Honesty I've seen my husband with his more traditional executive-type job also have the it's never done problem. That comes with the territory with any sort of growth and scale. I know several people in the indie business arena who are arguably more talented than myself but they were scared of having "outstanding work". I think it's very fair to say everyone has to find their own flow and business model but I'm still here having weathered many market storms thanks in a large part to being able to compartmentalize. If I didn't have the discipline to work when I needed to work, saying no to social things that weren't as important, or turn off my computer and stop checking orders when my family was home I would have burnt out long ago. I think this is a very important thing to remember. You can be the most talented person in the world, but if you don't have the work ethic or mindset to do what needs to be done when it needs to be done, it won't matter how talented you are.

We have to learn to safeguard our hearts and our energy. Not everyone and everything is for you all the time. It's cliche but some people or activities are just good for seasons. Really sit down and journal or pray about what you want and what is really important to you and then arrange as much of your life and energy around those things. Of course, you may not be able to make all of the big changes overnight with your schedule and life but start thinking how would the version of you who had that life feel and act. What would she do? Make your boundaries and standards off of that, even if at first it just seems like it's in your head. I truly think being an only child with a great imagination and somewhat delusional outlook has really come in handy here. I got a lot of practice thinking about how I wanted my life to be, with no one else around to influence me. I also got really good at setting goals and working towards them. It was actually pretty easy for me to make big changes in my life because it was just me taking on the challenge and pretending to myself that it was going to work out for my good somehow. This is similar to the idea of making friends with your inner monologue I spoke about in Chapter 5. Once you know who you want to be you can figure out the standards and boundaries that version of yourself would have and then start enforcing them. It's kind of like reverse engineering your own future. You slowly trick yourself into becoming your own most ideal version of yourself. No, I can't trick myself into becoming tall and narrow, but I can slowly become the best me that my body can support

9

Build your own business no pyramid required.

I am aware that this is turning out to be somewhat of a schizophrenic book. To me the topic of finding yourself, and starting a business are basically the same thing. I understand that this may not be how it is for everybody, but for me and many people, I know, creative expression doesn't end up being water coloring by a window, but rather building and creating a business, irregardless of scale. I honestly don't really think it matters. If what you're building is a tiny side hustle, that you love and enjoy, or a larger business with staff and more responsibilities. Honestly for me it definitely started out as one thing and grew into another and who knows where it will go as my life progresses. All I know is that the challenge and creativity of pulling something that I want to exist straight out of the ether is endlessly satisfying to me. I think there's a lot of self discovery to be found, and having to actually pin yourself down and add structure and monetization to something you care about. I think it's also important to be noted that I'm not saying that you have to turn all of your passions into a business. I definitely think it's important to have hobbies that are literally just for you. For me, I really enjoy yoga and exercise (also shopping for cute outfits for all of those activities but that's a topic for another day) those are activities that I pay for that are just for me that I enjoy and make my life and health better I have zero desire to monetize or teach any of those activities. For me the " yarn business" has become my business. Not to say that I don't thoroughly enjoy the many hobby aspects of the fiber arts, but that has definitely become my career. I'm sure there are many people you could find that would be the complete opposite who teach yoga or Pilates for trade and then love knitting or crochet as a hobby to relax. I think it's incredibly important to have both I think for many women, especially currently in the season where you are home with small children or in any situation where having a practical 9 to 5 job is not in the cards having something that you can pull out that creates even just a small amount of financial independence can be very empowering. For me having that little bit of extra money, that was just mine that I could spend on something I deemed frivolous that wasn't beneficial to our family was incredibly important. I've definitely been raised in the era of "don't you depend on a man" while simultaneously been told the importance of being home with my kids when they were little. This seemed like an impossible standard to try to hit. How do you fully embrace staying home and letting your life revolve around caring for your family and being committed to your family group as a whole versus a career while also having your own money, flexibility, and security?

Honestly, the best answer I have found this dilemma is to have some sort of a side hustle that you could have the option to build into more of a full-time career as your kids get older, or your family obligations change. I totally get that this may not be what lights everybody up but I'm also willing to bet that you're not reading this book if that doesn't at least sort of sound appealing to you. If you were wired a bit more for the 9 to 5, but you also would like more flexibility, I've definitely seen people be successful with many different remote work from home situation, such as medical coding or scheduling etc. I actually worked for a nationwide legal aid company as a client manager where I made my own hours and work from home for three years before I had kids. At the time I thought this was going to be the perfect job for me to transition and to continue working while staying home with babies. It turned out that God knew better, because this company tanked due to new management pretty much exactly the same time that I gave birth to my first child so I was forced to go back to the drawing board. In retrospect, I now see that there's no way I would've been able to do a good job of that job in the small amount of time that my baby was asleep. I am also a tremendous advocate for if you have a new baby taking some time off and really regroup later. I know I went through a real difficult phase postpartum and if I've been trying to make any sort of long-term life decisions about work or myself that definitely wouldn't have been the time to be doing it. One of the ways that entrepreneurship is more challenging than a regular 9 to 5 is it really does involve much more introspection and self-discipline. If you have just had a new baby, even if you think you're up to this, you probably shouldn't be. I know even now if I'm hungry or overly tired I'm probably going to make some pretty terrible decisions. So I'm going to assume that you are not a brand new mom with no help like I was and that your life has progressed to the point where you're ready to make some changes, Once you reach that point if you have the spark and personality for it Entrepreneurship can be one of the most rewarding, self soothing paths you can choose. I highly recommend reading the book, "The Entrepreneur Personality Type" by Alex Charfan. Just the introduction alone of that book completely explained, and validated my feelings I've had since high school I really feel like entrepreneurship really is best described as a personality type. It's either in your blood and it's undeniable or it's not. Honestly it's probably easier if it's not. Entrepreneurs writers and artists in my opinion are all kind of cut from the same cloth and our paths definitely overlap. As I'm sitting here writing this book while running a business that is based in the arts I can definitely validate this.

Signs of entrepreneurial personality type according to me.

A strong desire to build something and run something in your own way. To create something with a strong point of view.

An extreme boredom, and an intolerance of just trading your time for money doing repetitive task.

Not being appeased into doing what you would consider boring or repetitive work for the sake of sociability. You are probably not that person who doesn't mind folding sweaters all day because you like talking to the other employees you're probably the person that is dying to go home and do something you actually find valuable or engaging.

Always kind of feeling like you have some sort of mission that you're working on even if that mission is just make more dollar bills to buy more stuff that you want. You are the lemonade stand kid, or the person who is always looking for a way to monetize what they enjoy doing.

You're probably a bit of a weirdo, you are often alone with your own thoughts and ideas, and are generally confused with the masses.

You've probably been diagnosed with ADHD or had people try to diagnose you at least.

You were probably not the world's greatest student.

Chronic daydreamer.

You probably have always had this weird underline feeling that you just don't fit in to the world in the same way, that most of your peers do.

You have often been concerned that you are selfish because you want to live life on your own terms

If this sounds like you, I am here to cheer you along in starting to scratch that itch. I'm not saying you have to become the next Richard Branson. I'm just saying that you may find much more Validation, self growth and work life balance through betting on yourself, than through trying to fit in with others. If you are in the even more fortunate position to where you actually have some extra time and flexibility in your life due to also being a stay at home, mom or " housewife" dare I say then you are in a tremendously advantageous position to be able to really double down on yourself. If your income is not necessarily needed to support a family , then why not really give yourself permission to try at what it is your heart desires, and learn how to turn that desire into money even if it's just a little bit of money when you start. Put that money somewhere for yourself let it be a rainy day fund. Your, my kids really want to go on this trip fund, your security, your shopping money. It's what our grandmothers would've called coffee can money little bit of cash they could scrape together doing odd jobs from their specialities or just money, saved and put aside that no one would miss. Now, of course I'm not saying you have to do it this way. I have definitely enjoyed having my income supplement our family income over the years. I was just relating back to earlier in this chapter when I said I was raised that you were supposed to be independent and look after yourself while also trying to achieve a flexible lifestyle to prioritize your family role. I have simply just not found a better way to do this. I would like to emphasize that this choice could look very different for different people. It could be real estate it could be selling your wares online, becoming an author or yoga instructor , a tutor an online teacher, the possibilities really are endless.

10

Chase your passion and take no shit

One of my favorite quotes from one of my favorite people is from my Aunt Susan she always told me that "The first shovel shit someone throws your way you better throw it right back or they'll keep it coming". Now I'm not here to debate, whether or not that was a appropriate advice to give eight-year-old me, but it has definitely proven to be good advice that I have already passed onto my girls. You absolutely can't go through life making everyone happy or having everyone approve of you. Now I know this is something we have all heard 100 times so here I am telling you again. This is something I have to tell myself every single day it seems to be human nature to want to be liked an approved of but there's just so many people with so many different opinions on what is good and approvable it's just never going to happen. No matter what path you choose. There's always going to be people both vocal and silently giving you the stink eye who don't approve of what you're wearing how you're living or what you're spending your money on. I spent way too many years trying to walk that type rope down the middle where you didn't ruffle too many feathers on one side or the other. I absolutely hate being in an environment full of conflict so this is definitely an urge I deeply understand. I would say once I hit my 30s and had more demands on my energy level and time that definitely put my ability to give a shit into a much finer point. I have to say this is one of my favorite things about getting older is you really do reach this point where you just kind of don't care nearly as much about what other people think of you. I feel like I'm at the sweet spot where I'm young enough to still wear what I want and go where I want while still being old enough to not need anyone's permission or approval. I personally hope this feeling continues for the rest of forever. Besides, just getting older and wiser, having my own business has intensified this feeling. You kind of get forced into having to be your own brand. This was definitely something I avoided strongly, for let's say the first eight years of owning a business. I went through many phases with my website and social media presence. I kept trying to take myself out of the equation and make it this standalone brand that didn't necessarily have anything to do with me. I tried putting the focus on our staff, on our community on our Facebook group or our farmers and suppliers, but when the going got tough, and the economy started crashing and small businesses started getting their asses handed to them left and right it became very apparent that my business was me and without my personality, backbone and general determination, it wasn't going to continue to be here. This made me have to kind of look at myself more as a brand for as annoying as that sounds. This level of introspection is not always comfortable, but can be oddly therapeutic. I have to say, accepting that I have to be the spokes person and figurehead of my own business, just like the owner of a bakery would be connected with the brand of the shop and the treats within has been a real learning experience for me. Being forced to step more into your own branding and look more closely at yourself can really help to put your life and values under a microscope. I personally have found building a brand that I'm happy with has directly lead to helping me build a life that I am happy with. Something that may be tremendously, important or attractive to one person may not be necessarily for you. The final outcome is of course much more of a journey versus a destination and is going to look different for everyone.

11

End struggle mom culture

I really encourage you to continuously ask yourself "What do I want?' I really think so many of us honestly don't know. We're too busy just reacting to life to pick a direction or goal. It doesn't have to be anything big or monumental. Just always beware of what you actually want. Are you even hungry right now? Are you starving and need to just eat something nourishing instead of being in a terrible mood pushing through? Do you want different responsibilities to raise your kids or home school? Do you need something to build and create that's more than just playdates or cubicle time? Do you want to have more time to work out or maybe you need more sleep? You see how this question can go on and on. All of this started for me because I wanted an extra $100 a month to get a pedicure now and then or save up for a trip with my husband. That was a clear enough goal for me though and it started the domino effect that got me here. I am by no means writing this from some shiny pentacle of success. I'm just a mom on a laptop. I hope to keep riding this ride for as long as I can. I can tell you that every single year I've worked for myself I've grown and learned and become happier. Even in the years that looked like a setback thanks to a tanking economy when I did the books and reflected the business actually grew, or got leaner, more profitable, and focused. I do know that I am 100% not who I was trying to find my purpose and validation in other people's careers and businesses, or the pale, puffy mom with low self-worth. I don't know why as women it's so painful to admit that we should probably like ourselves. We don't even know how to take a compliment. As soon as someone says something nice we start making up excuses for why they shouldn't. You can be grounded and somewhat delusional at the same time. You can think you're pretty fabulous and worthy of a nice life while also knowing that you may not be society's current standard of beauty or intelligence. I'm going to call it fear of lipstick-on a pig syndrome. When you are afraid that if you "dress cute" or " try something new" you'll look foolish and your peers will all whisper who is she to wear that, try that etc? We're so afraid that we're the pig and that any efforts to live in a more aligned way with what our heart wants will just make it so painfully obvious to the world how lacking we are. I may step on some toes here but can we please, please kill off this toxic "struggle mom" " struggle millennial" and " struggle marriage" bull shit. Now I love coffee, wine, dry shampoo, and motherhood as much as the next lady probably even more. Those are basically the pillars of my existence. I also love wearing leggings or joggers for most occasions but ya'll we can branch out. The dirty hair, "mom life, mama bear" shirts. We can all have interests and passions outside of " not before my coffee" and " rose' all day" slogans. Little Braighleigh or Carter Cash will be just fine if you need some sleep and a green smoothie or maybe some fresh air. The whole day doesn't have to revolve around what will make your man or your kids most happy. They will just ignore you and take you for granted if you just keep reducing yourself to a shadow in the corner. You will have a harder time being taken seriously even by yourself if you're never even a little demanding. Life can suck, kids are hard, and trying to afford anything right now is the worst. I'm not saying be reckless but within your current life and means take a few small stands for the person you want to be. Buy some nail polish or new E.L.F makeup (it's so cheap and nice I think) Tell the kids you will be putting on the show you want to watch instead of reruns of whatever horrible crap they have been blasting for hours nonstop. They can learn to color or get on board with learning about cooking on the Great British Baking Show or whatever you are watching. Make what you want for dinner and let everyone else figure it out. Especially if you already asked for people's input and were told they don't care. Perfect that means you get to do what you want. Husband in a bad mood about nothing that has anything to do with you? Go do something fun you want to do even if it's just finding the perfect hair color/bang combo or garden layout on Pinterest. Try to dream big, envision the life you want and the person you want to be, and move towards it. If you do have kids especially girls like I do, ask yourself when they are grown do you want them dimming themselves down just to fit in with the "struggle life narrative" to be easily accepted by all the masses of drifting complainers? Like Neapolitan Hill writes in one of my favorite books " Outwitting the Devil" You have to make a stand for your goals and your life and not get sucked into being a drifter. Drifting along with the unhappy masses trapped in constant disappointment, too busy looking at their phones and shuffling feet to see the sky and the horizon. Don't get sucked into complacency. Be too much. Be spoiled and loud.

92

Stand for what you want even if right now that's just a matcha latte. Expect to have a good day whether it's snuggling with your babies and going for a walk or making some great moves in whatever endeavor you choose. Shit is going to happen but don't let it mean anything. Let it be nothing and cast it off. If it's a major tragedy that you must deal with throw yourself fully into feeling it and learning the lessons you need to but if it's just some petty bullshit let it go. When people let you down walk away if they are just fake friends. Save the real fight for relationships for the ones closest to you who need the most grace. I will wrap up this rant by reminding you of the saying that you become most like the 5 people you spend time with. I think this is so true. Don't let those 5 people all be small-minded people just because of the environment you are in. Go find podcasts, influencers, authors, YouTubers, pastors, and business leaders, and then spend time taking in their energy and vibes. That will slowly start to change your life.

12

Technology for Good

I know I know we've all watched too many sci-fi movies where technology eventually ends up, outgrowing us and taking over the world. I am, however, an eternal optimist, and I definitely love all of my technology gadgets, including the pink I Mac that I'm currently writing this on. For someone with many learning disabilities, such as myself having technology to help me streamline my thoughts and get things edited correctly can be a lifesaver. Some of my favorite techno lifesavers are

The talk-to-text feature for spelling and writing as quickly as my mind moves and my fingers can't keep up.

Auto text inserts for keyboard shortcuts to not have to look up that weblink that I post everywhere but can't remember the lengthy URL Slug.

Photo syncing and the Cloud. My work and my life overlap so much of the time that being able to take pictures or write down notes on the fly in between everything else that I'm doing for myself or my family lets me be able to easily find it back at my desktop when I return home.

Spell check, enough said.

Social media auto schedulers. So many options are available today I am currently using Tailwind but I know that Facebook and Insta business pages just came out with some sort of built-in feature with AI copywriting and scheduling. I haven't looked into it too much because I was already set up and running for multiple brands on Tailwind.

If you already have a busy life and you're just looking to fit in your new venture in between the moving pieces of your life then technology is your friend. I'm always amazed by how many people I run into in the entrepreneurial sphere who seem to be completely resistant to the idea of learning how to do anything new with technology. I get it, I am an elder millennial I remember not wanting to have a cell phone in high school because I thought it meant my Dad was just trying to keep tabs on me. I was very resistant to text messages and thought emoticons were the devil. I have completely changed my tune and pretty much communicate with people via messenger or text with hieroglyphic-style pictures at this point. What can I say without the laughing face after my messages people would not get that I am joking and think I'm just a bitch. So this being said unless you are prepared to only work in a physical lemonade stand style of business that promotes only via word of mouth you may want to look at what's out there. Also for the love of everything good please look into getting the extended I cloud storage. If you end up being like me and taking so many videos and movies of everything from your next marketing plan to your kid's basketball game then you will love not having to delete things just to send them to yourself. It amazes me how far I've come with this. When I first started my husband convinced me that I needed to have a YouTube channel to highlight the brand of spinning wheel that I have for sale on my website. I REALLY didn't want to do this. I had no clue how to make all the cute jump-cut edits or even what that was. I was not someone who loved taking pictures or videos of myself (something I've had to get over) and I had an old ass I Phone with a sort of wonky camera. You can tell from some of my first videos that the background seems to move around sort of like I'm in a fishbowl. There are comments complaining and everything. To film and then post a video I would have to first delete every single picture or video off of my phone. Then use some really old " Go Pro" app to spice the clips together. 9 times out of 10 my phone would then crash and I'd have to offload most of my apps to get it to save and then somehow get it on YouTube after that. Then I could delete my video and go back to using my phone like normal. So when I tell you how much I love all of the extra memory and aids and quicker processing speeds I have now I don't just say that to sound spoiled. The amount of angst and time that these little tricks and aids saved me is worth the investment every time. You have to launch ugly. Start where you have to start, use what you have but when you can start adding new tools to your arsenal please do, and then write it off on your taxes! It doesn't even have to be just throwing money at problems just a little bit of research on a topic can be empowering. I get asked lots of " How do I do...." Kind of questions and while I don't mind helping people most of the time all I going to do is look up the exact question on Google or YouTube and then chase down that rabbit hole. That's how I know any and everything. Just being curious and open-minded. Having a vague idea of what I think the ideal solution would be and then trying to find the tool or app that will help make that happen. Half the time there is a shortcut or tool that will fix my problem already loaded onto my computer I just have to know the right button to push. Instead of feeling helpless or playing dumb just get to looking up your questions. Lord help me if the government ever decides to search my computer for search queries because I've logged hundreds of random questions by this point.

13

It can be a lonely road

One thing One thing that sucks but I feel like it needs to be addressed is that while you're going on this journey of self-evolution it's going to get lonely. Lonely is something I'm pretty familiar with as an only child who never really fit in in the town I grew up in. I have always had that feeling of being a bit of an outsider, no matter where I go, and I've have kind of learned to embrace and deal with that. I enjoy having my own time, and I need space to be creative and think straight. As I'm writing this, my whole family has been snowed in for what feels like an eternity here in East Tennessee. This has given me plenty of opportunity to look at my own needs between the need to be around people and laugh and enjoy their energy also very much need time to myself to hold a cup of coffee and stare off and space until I get my mojo going in the right direction. I don't have many female friends and I know online there's lots of discourse about how women who don't have many female friends are some sort of a red flag. I would like to preface this was saying the reason I don't have many female friends isn't, because I'm some sort of toxic pick me chick who's out to get everyone's man. It's much more that I have a very hard time maintaining surface level friendships and interest. In my experience this seems to be a large part of female friendships. Throw in a handful of trust issues on top of that and there you go. I'm old enough to recognize a cycle in my own life with this where I will have a group of friends and try my best to fit into what the group is up to but then, as I evolve into the next version of myself I no longer can stay there. I've done this with friends in high school, friends from college and Mom friends in my current life. The good news is from each of these phases I've managed to pick up at least one friendship that I have taken with me into the future. So I guess it's not true to say I don't have female friends it's probably more accurate to say I don't have many female friends who live within driving distance of my house. I just wanted to give you this as sort of a warning that, as you dig into more of what makes you happy you may end up with a smaller social circle. It sucks but it seems to be necessary. After you go through whatever growth phase, or incubation that you need to go through, you will come out, even if you don't really realize it as a different better version of yourself who has integrated some life lessons, and is now embodied more of the person that you want to be. This version of you will then make new friends and social circles that will fit better so you just have to hold onto that idea. I think it's damaging and unhelpful to try to hold onto relationships that are no longer fitting into your life or people that are no longer respectful to you. So many women get trapped in the cycle of being nice. I hate the idea of being nice I would much rather be kind than nice. People aren't going to like you and they're going to talk shit about you no matter what. So you might as well be true to who you want to be, and what feels best and most aligned to you, and standing with your own moral code. This holds especially true if you start being successful in either your personal life or business. If you have a relationship that's doing great and you can afford to do all the things that you want to do People are going to be jealous and talk bad about you and you're happiness. If you have a business that you've built that you're proud of that starts making money and gives you the freedom to live your life and be flexible and devoted to your family. People are going to talk shit because you didn't take the common path and they say that you have things that they don't. Lord, help you if you manage to have both, then you're just leaving yourself wide open for other peoples jealousy, and insecurities. This is something I'm still walking through right now that's probably half the reason I'm writing this book I need to feel like there are other people out there who are like me I'm excited for you. I wish we could be friends in real life because it gets lonely out there. Synopsis I guess my point with this is being true to yourself and your loved ones and family unit will always be more important than making yourself small , bite-sized and acceptable for all the bitches out there.

I think more people need to make friends with their feelings of jealousy and envy. I heard on a podcast the idea that when you see someone or something that stirs, jealousy or envy instead of going with the baser urge to not like them or talk shit about the in your head about how you think they don't deserve it or you deserve it more, etc. you should look at what is it that they embody or have that you want. That's just God or the universe showing you. Hey, this is one of your next desires.. here's a goal you should work towards. It's funny because from our point of view, everyone would want the same thing, but we all want different things and are jealous of different things. For one person, it may be the corner, office career, recognition, and doing something really great in their industry. Instead of hating that person in your head, you need to learn to be more like them and get your own corner, office, and job recognition. You have just been given the gift of knowing that you are created to be a leader and not just a cog in a box. One thing that I didn't realize was that so many people really just want to be a cog in a box. It always blows my mind to realize this because that's not how I'm wired at all. It took me years to realize that having the entrepreneurial leadership spark and the desire to walk your own path, lead and innovate is definitely not something that most people have. But that's good news. We need people to just do their job and stay in their lane. It's not that they are bad or dumb or wrong. It's just that their dream is something totally different and that part of their life is just a small corner of what makes them happy and not a major goal like it would be for you. For somebody else, it may be the lady on vacation with the expensive luggage and the nice jewelry who looks like she's going somewhere fabulous. Let's be real that's the person I'm jealous of. Younger me would've looked at someone like that and been like man It must be nice to be that bitch where life just works out for you. I know that it's really that I would like to have a life filled with beauty, excitement and travel while living in a body that seems well taken care of and magnetic. I want freedom, time and beauty in my own life. That woman to me would've represented someone who was cherished, respected, and powerful in her circle. So when you look at it like that, the vacation woman would be a guidepost, not someone to be envious of. She's someone to be thanked. Track down the feeling that is making you jealous to the source and then start plotting your own path to get those things God has just shown you something that you're meant to go after.

Conclusion :
  Making Peace with Yourself

It's also worth noting It's also worth noting that I don't think anyone ever truly feels like they have made it to the person they want to be. I know if me from 20 years ago could see me now they would be super impressed however currently it just feels like living life with the usual ups and downs and personal aggravations with myself daily. If your goal is just partly business, then you just have to start taking those first steps towards what you want to do there is absolutely no way to avoid being terrible at first. Thanks, Facebook for constantly reminding me of what I was posting 10 years ago. I will always be equally horrified and impressed with my first attempts at "business". It would be easy to beat myself up about how terrible some of my early copy and images look but I also have to remember that I basically had no clue what I was doing and that technology has come a long way. Just like fashion styles business styles always change, so you just kinda have to jump on the merry-go-round and figure it out as you go. The amount of things that have changed cyclically since I started working would blow your mind. Things have gone from webinars to online summit events to Evergreen funnels to a TikTok shop. Instagram alone has changed its algorithm at least 200 times. There is absolutely no good time to either start a family or start a business. You just have to want to do it and jump in. The trick is to try not to beat yourself up too badly. No one else is watching what you're doing nearly as closely as you are anyway. The people who are watching are most likely impressed you're trying anything at all even if they don't say it. This is the exact same advice that I was given about when to start having kids there's no good time, there's never enough money. It will work out in the end though. We all only get one go at this life, so if you really want to pursue either of those things, you have to just start living as the person who is already doing them now. That sounds like the world's most annoying advice and it's something I struggle with every day but it really does work pretty much just like magic. Figure out what it is that you want and then figure out what you can do or think or change about yourself right now to feel more like that's currently happening or yours. Find something anything to be grateful for. Be grateful there's food in your house, be grateful your family is healthy, be grateful your Internet connection is strong. Be grateful for your friends, even if you just have one. Most importantly stop waiting for permission from your parents, your husband, society, your friend group or whoever to be who you want to be. No fairy is going to show up and wave a wand and declare that you are now smart or pretty enough to have the life that you want. There's no nice way about it you just have to fix what you can fix and then try to accept and love what you can't.

Practical Indie business resources

Product lines, Email funnels and becoming luxe online

Up to this point, I've talked a lot about why I think starting your own business is such an important component of achieving the flexible lifestyle you are after. I however have not given you any solid practical steps. One thing that always annoys me is when I pick up a book really hoping to get some brass tacks directions and then it's all just fluff. That was one thing I was really paranoid about when I started this project. I didn't want to feel like I was tossing a bucket of water into the ocean of similar content. However, after 10 years of trying to hone my skills, I have some strong opinions about things.

One of the first lessons I learned that helped to set me apart from other online craft businesses way back when I was selling knitwear on Etsy was to start using product lines both seasonal and year-round. If you think about it product lines are EVERYWHERE.

I personally love shopping for all the girly stuff, we all have our vises. No matter if you're into Stanley cups, yoga pants, the latest book series, or the landscaping craze I'm willing to bet if you check out the brand's marketing they have a repeating baseline and fun seasonal collections. Seriously just go walk around Target. I honestly follow the marketing of a few brands that I particularly enjoy shopping from, but I also to study their marketing.

Both YETI and SKIMS are great examples of having a really solid baseline that people love shopping from all the time for foundations with fun rotating seasonal colors or options. If you're just starting out, especially in more of a handmade or creative business, it can be really easy to just start making one-offs of things that you like and then listing them for sale. While this may work on a small scale with people who already know, would love you are just excited to buy from you. If you're trying to create anything sustainable, you need to be able to be known for something and that's where your core product line needs to come in. Once you design and iron out all of the details of the process of keeping your core product line moving, you can move on to creating fun seasonal lines. Examples of this could be special colors, special fabrics, or textures. Special accessories or branding depending on what it is that you sell. This would be most important if you are building a brand and a company for either physical or digital products. I also see how this could work if you were even just reselling things on Amazon you might want to start with a focus on, for example, anti-aging supplements that you were reselling and then work seasonal trendy items around the holidays that shoppers are searching for. That is not something I have personally done. You can definitely see how many Amazon sellers use this technique and copy it if that's the route you want to go.

The second major lesson that I learned was about email lists and email funnels. At the time that I'm writing this book this definitely seems like a less revolutionary concept than it did to me when I was starting out because it seems like you can't do anything without ending up going through some sort of an email funnel, but this is something that many entrepreneurs or start-up small businesses really miss on the front end. Even if you feel silly and like you're not nearly big or important enough to need an email list, you really need to start one. There are so many options out there that are easy to start out with. I know I started out with MailChimp which I know has changed a good bit over the years but I imagine if you google free email list you can probably get started for not much. The reason it's important to have an email list not just followers on Instagram, YouTube, etc. is all of the social media platforms that you are comfortable with now are going to change at at least 100 times and let you down even more in just a handful of years. It's also very misleading on how popular or well a brand may be doing. I know for myself in the Fiber Arts on Instagram in particular, there always seem to be certain business accounts or influencers that could post a picture of a drink sitting on a table and everyone loses their mind about it millions of likes comments, shares, etc. I can make a post that I think is a beautiful and informative post and no one sees it. However, I don't feel too bad about this because I know that in my particular niche, my website actually has great organic search-ability and my subscriptions are always growing despite not being a social media darling. I owe this in large part to my email list, email campaigns, and funnels. People may never see what I post on social media but they do get my emails about my product lines being restocked and new offers that are available and that drives sales, not the other way around. I have changed tracks so many times and while that is always awkward, I'm always able to email my list and let them know where we're moving to and what those changes are so it doesn't impact my bottom line.

Thirdly the idea of being seen as Luxe online is also known as good branding. Everyone loves to say beauty is only skin deep, and you shouldn't judge a book by its cover, etc. that all sounds great and is well and good, but when it comes to the land of Internet, marketing, and e-commerce, looking polished and not giving people eyeball shock or bad vibes is incredibly important. Think about it we spend a lot of time looking at buying random boring things off of Amazon like lint rollers, dog bowls, toilet paper, all the things. Our eyes have gotten very used to looking at things with clear imaging on a white background for the most part so then all of a sudden you're looking at jewelry and somebody has handmade earrings hanging on the side of a chalk-painted cheese, grater, or something even if you logically get that they were going for like a shabby chic look your brain is going to think this is a cheap piece of crap and probably not want to buy it. Nothing makes me crazier than seeing other small business owners complain about the unfairness of e-commerce and how no one is buying what they are selling and then I click over to their website and it has zero useful product description and all of their pictures look like it was taken on their grandmother's Afghan on their sofa at 10:30 at night under a bad yellow 60 W lightbulb. And I know you think I'm joking right now, but I promise I've seen this exact setup time and time again accompanying someone whining about the unfairness of the market. People are not going to buy things from you or take you seriously online if what you are presenting is such a total contradiction from how we are used to shopping online. I've seen the same thing, but in the opposite extreme of too much thought and effort being put into images where everything is overly cutesy or Photoshopped, or has some sort of theme with graphics in the background, while I love a good theme, and definitely have lots of images that have wooden tables, granite, fabric etc. in the background of product images. I always have white background images for the main website pages. As I had mentioned earlier, I have gone through many phases with branding and really tried to keep the brand separate from my own personal taste, or aesthetic because I know I'm not everyone's cup of tea. However, what has felt most authentic to me as far as branding goes, was really to look at it almost like I would my own personal style and getting dressed. I gravitate towards maybe two neutrals and an accent. Same with fonts, two basics, and an accent, and then let it really feel like you. Repeat these themes over and over again in your images, logos, emails, etc. There really is something to be said for everything kind of matching like outfits. This is something I've really come to appreciate more in the past 10 years of my own wardrobe. I used to have lots of different tops and bottoms that I picked up out of the clearance section and figured I was cool enough to figure out how to make interesting outfits out of them, and that worked out most of the time it definitely led to decision fatigue on a regular basis. Last time, I got mad at my closet and pulled everything out and re-organized it. I followed a friend's advice. She said especially with athleisure-type outfits to actually hang them together in matching groups on the same coat hanger so I could easily pick up one basically monochromatic outfit and be about my day. You can really say the same thing for branding. I use the same email templates over and over again I have the same look and feel to my social media post so even if my brand is pink and sparkly and maximalist I feel it's at least matching and coordinated because it's consistent. Think about it even though Apple products come in a wide range of colors and models when we think of Apple branding, most of us, think of those extremely sturdy white boxes that we are afraid to throw away with the minimalist white Apple logo.

So now I know what you're thinking that's all well and good but how do you get "fans" to get on my email list to even see this great marketing? I just told you that I had given up "being popular " in certain areas online so what's the trick? In my experience, there is a lot of smoke and mirrors online. I'm not saying I'm the biggest name in any particular area but the people who resonate with me are a fantastic online community who all jive and encourage each other. Here is a little lesson I picked up from personal experience. I sell online courses on my website and while at the time of writing this, they are not the top seller from month to month but they are something I'm proud of. One day I was contacted by the owner of another fiber arts business that from my point of view was " way bigger " than my brand was. She wanted to sell courses on similar topics on her website and wanted to work with other creators in a collaboration of sorts where she would host and promote them and there was some sort of money splitting. I honestly don't remember too many of the details because it clearly didn't work out. While emailing back in forth about this plan of hers she mentioned the size of her email list as a way to I guess entice people to want to be promoted through her brand. I was really surprised because it was less than half the size of mine at the time. I was shocked because in my imagination her brand was so much larger and " more successful" than mine. As it turns it she didn't like my videos which I didn't care about because my courses match the style of my YouTube Chanel which has proven to be a success so I wasn't planning on changing. I in turn was not impressed with her marketing reach or audience because I felt that despite her brand being more popular in certain Facebook groups my brand clearly had more reach and conversion. This was an eye-opener for me that you can't always judge the successes or profitability of the brands you are comparing yourself to on social media. I don't mean any of this mean. This brand is fabulous and I'm sure performing way better than me in some areas, my takeaway was to not discount my own work despite online popularity. My website and branding, while there is always room for improvement translates as an established professional brand and that has really helped to snowball my sales and searchability online. If you want to grow your email list you need to have some sort of an offer on your website that people will sign up to get like a coupon, e-book, special offer, etc. Then if your email platform allows you can set up a few automated emails to go out to people with info that they will genuinely find helpful and endear you to them. Another common email list fear is that if you email too much you will bother people and they will unsubscribe. You want to send out good content that people enjoy getting and that way the people who really jive with you will fall more in love with what you do and the people you aren't right for WILL unsubscribe and that way you don't end up having an email list full of people who don't like what you're about. You will end up with a healthier email list and as you grow and end up paying to send emails(by size of recipients) to people who will just mark you for spam.

To recap the tips covered in this chapter. First, you want to plot out a brand you can get behind even if it's as simple as " Designs by (your name)" or whatever. Then design a classic product line full of whatever it is that you want to be known for on a repeatable basis of services or products. After you've ironed that out you can start rotating in smaller seasonal lines to keep people excited and move them in and out with sales and promotions to your email list! That's the second part is to set up an email list with some sort of coupon offer to get people to join. Then you just keep all this going with consistent branding with quality images and content that seems natural and alluring to you. I know that seems like a lot but I promise once you get a product line and a vibe nailed down it really does all grow on itself over time. Also, keep in mind that nothing stays static forever. My brand has grown and changed so much over the years but at a gradual enough pace that it has felt mostly organic.

Mindset
  Arguably the most important part
  I can't really think of anything more important to tell you than mindset. I'm sitting here writing and I can tell that this is nearing the end of this particular book. I can already tell that many of these topics I'm itching to expand on in other conversations and future books. I don't want to overwhelm you with too much info at one time. I'm trying to imagine

who you are reading this book. What your most immediate goals would be? I named this book " Entrepreneurial Trophy Wife" as a joke but also in an effort to appeal to women who wanted to be both appreciated and free in their families as well as whatever part of the business world they choose. I think it's natural to want people to notice and appreciate our efforts in all aspects of our lives but more than that to have the freedom to fund and structure our lives the way we see fit. To me achieving a level of freedom and prosperity where you can make your own rules while having enough flexibility and happiness to really show up as the best version of yourself for the people you love is the ultimate goal. I am proud to say that for me at least I'm in a small way already living out these dreams for myself and I'm grateful every day. That's my main reason for writing this book is in the small hope that it might help someone else get to that sweet spot in their own life. I can't tell you what exactly your dream girl experience is for your life but I can tell you that if you get clear to yourself on what that dream girl life would be and then really lean into listening to that still small voice in your head that you'll be a lot closer than you think. I personally think all women are a little magic. I think we are the energy source and powerhouse to so many people in our lives even if we don't notice.

Men may always want to think they are the captain of the ship but where would they be without the constant motor of the women in their lives? We need to learn to not just inspire and motivate the people we love but more importantly use our own power to fuel our own dreams. We have so much power to pull things straight out of the ether that so many of us never even realize. Write down who and what you want your life to be, pray, or search your soul for answers on your next right step towards that. Even if it's just go take a shower and wash your face, drink more water, and learn a new skill. In my case just keep typing one more badly misspelled sentence after another. Believe it or not, it'll all string together and equal something better. Remember the more little victories you can prove to your own subconscious the more you'll start to trust yourself. Stop feeling like you're taking up too much space or being someone you're not. Everyone feels fake to an extent. Be the main character in your own life. So many people play small if you're even a little brave you'll be ahead of the pack. I think that's where I'll end this one. Just keep being a little brave. I watch my daughters in elementary school every day have to be a little brave at something new. It's easy for me to tell them to take no shit from the mean lunch lady but that's a big deal when your a little kid. Every day they try new things and keep going even if they're nervous and I know that they get some of that nerve from me. I know that they are seeing me do scary or new things and I'm still here to tell about it. You can too. Trust me.

After thoughts

Thank you for reading this book! This has been the new brave thing I've been working on for over a year now and I'm terrified and thrilled to think that anyone would have read to this point. If you want to shoot me an email you can find me at erin@feralscene.com You can find me on all the socials as either ErinSJames , FeralScene or Craftyhousewifeyarns or some combination of both. I have a prolific YouTube Channel that will have info on indie business and the fiber arts come find me for either. I also have an ever-growing collection of crafting subscriptions and online courses for fiber arts and coming soon indie business topics like this book. Let me know what you'd like to know more about. You can also find my podcast in all the places.

About the Author

Erin James lives with her family in Knoxville TN.

She is an Entrepreneur at heart. Anthropologist and Arts Curator

She is married to her favorite person and loves being a mom more than anything.

My adventures in working, marriage, kids, losing myself, finding myself, actually making friends with women, evolving, building a successful business, yoga, gin, pissing off people, and being happy on my terms

While this book is not for everyone it is for those who want some real-life advice about...

- Working and being a mom of young children.
- This dumb idea that you have to be just one thing.
- The weird phobia of admitting that you're a work from home mom.
- Guilt over having self-esteem and boundaries (I prefer to call them standards)
- Practical how-to's for building your own "handmade" business no pyramid scheme required.
- Chasing your passion
- Remembering you're still a person and you can become a new version of yourself any time you want.
- Utilizing technology to rediscover the old-timey notion that you can have a family and make money all by yourself without waiting on anyone's permission.
- Taking no Shit.
- Finally making peace with yourself (most of the time).
- Embracing Your Authenticity as an Indie Entrepreneur or Artist

Join the author and entrepreneur as she dives deep into the world of indie entrepreneurship and artistic endeavors, unraveling the complex journey of self-discovery and professional success. Through a blend of personal anecdotes, practical advice, and powerful strategies, Feral offers a roadmap for embracing your unique voice and carving a path that aligns with your authentic self.

From overcoming self-doubt and societal expectations to harnessing creative energy and developing a strong personal brand, this book empowers you to break free from the confines of conformity and forge your path in the competitive landscape of entrepreneurship and artistry.

Let Feral guide you towards embracing your unique talents, finding your niche, and creating a sustainable and fulfilling career on your terms.

Discover how to tap into your unique strengths, cultivate an unapologetic mindset, and optimize your entrepreneurial path. From developing a standout personal brand to navigating the ever-evolving digital landscape, this book provides the essential tools and strategies you need to thrive as an indie entrepreneur or artist.

If you're ready to step off the beaten path and embrace the untamed journey of professional and personal growth, Feral is the definitive guide you need to unleash your true potential and thrive in the fiercely creative world of indie entrepreneurship and artistry.

Erin James lives with her family in Knoxville TN. She is an Entrepreneur at heart, Anthropologist and Art Curator.
She is married to her favorite person and loves being a mom more than anything.

Epilogue

Practical Indie Business Resources

Product lines, Email funnels and becoming luxe online

Up to this point, I've talked a lot about why I think starting your own business is such an important component of achieving the flexible lifestyle you are after. I however have not given you any solid practical steps. One thing that always annoys me is when I pick up a book really hoping to get some brass tacks directions and then it's all just fluff. That was one thing I was really paranoid about when I started this project. I didn't want to feel like I was tossing a bucket of water into the ocean of similar content. However, after 10 years of trying to hone my skills, I have some strong opinions about things.

One of the first lessons I learned that helped to

set me apart from other online craft businesses way back when I was selling knitwear on Etsy was to start using product lines both seasonal and year-round. If you think about it product lines are EVERYWHERE.

I personally love shopping for all the girly stuff, we all have our vises. No matter if you're into Stanley cups, yoga pants, the latest book series, or the landscaping craze I'm willing to bet if you check out the brand's marketing they have a repeating baseline and fun seasonal collections. Seriously just go walk around Target. I honestly follow the marketing of a few brands that I particularly enjoy shopping from, but I also to study their marketing. Both YETI and SKIMS are great examples of having a really solid baseline that people love shopping from all the time for foundations with fun rotating seasonal colors or options. If you're just starting out, especially in more of a handmade or creative business, it can be really easy to just start making one-offs of things that you like and then listing them for sale. While this may work on a small scale with people who already know, would love you are just excited to buy from you. If you're trying to create anything sustainable, you need to be able to be known for something and that's where your core product line needs to come in. Once you design and iron out all of the details of the process of keeping your core product line moving, you can move on to creating fun seasonal lines. Examples of this could be special colors, special fabrics, or textures. Special accessories or branding depending on what it is that you sell. This would be most important if you are building a brand and a company for either physical or digital products. I also see how this could work if you were even just reselling things on Amazon you might want to start with a focus on, for example, anti-aging supplements that you were reselling and then work seasonal trendy items around the holidays that shoppers are searching for. That is not something I have personally done. You can definitely see how many Amazon sellers use this technique and copy it if that's the route you want to go.

The second major lesson that I learned was about email lists and email funnels. At the time that I'm writing this book this definitely seems like a less revolutionary concept than it did to me when I was starting out because it seems like you can't do anything without ending up going through some sort of an email funnel, but this is something that many entrepreneurs or start-up small businesses really miss on the front end. Even if you feel silly and like you're not nearly big or important enough to need an email list, you really need to start one.

There are so many options out there that are easy to start out with. I know I started out with MailChimp which I know has changed a good bit over the years but I imagine if you google free email list you can probably get started for not much. The reason it's important to have an email list not just followers on Instagram, YouTube, etc. is all of the social media platforms that you are comfortable with now are going to change at at least 100 times and let you down even more in just a handful of years. It's also very misleading on how popular or well a brand may be doing. I know for myself in the Fiber Arts on Instagram in particular, there always seem to be certain business accounts or influencers that could post a picture of a drink sitting on a table and everyone loses their mind about it millions of likes comments, shares, etc. I can make a post that I think is a beautiful and informative post and no one sees it. However, I don't feel too bad about this because I know that in my particular niche, my website actually has great organic search-ability and my subscriptions are always growing despite not being a social media darling. I owe this in large part to my email list, email campaigns, and funnels. People may never see what I post on social media but they do get my emails about my product lines being restocked and new offers that are available and that drives sales, not the other way around. I have changed tracks so many times and while that is always awkward, I'm always able to email my list and let them know where we're moving to and what those changes are so it doesn't impact my bottom line.

Thirdly the idea of being seen as Luxe online is also known as good branding. Everyone loves to say beauty is only skin deep, and you shouldn't judge a book by its cover, etc. that all sounds great and is well and good, but when it comes to the land of Internet, marketing, and e-commerce, looking polished and not giving people eyeball shock or bad vibes is incredibly important. Think about it we spend a lot of time looking at buying random boring things off of Amazon like lint rollers, dog bowls, toilet paper, all the things. Our eyes have gotten very used to looking at things with clear imaging on a white background for the most part so then all of a sudden you're looking at jewelry and somebody has handmade earrings hanging on the side of a chalk-painted cheese, grater, or something even if you logically get that they were going for like a shabby chic look your brain is going to think this is a cheap piece of crap and probably not want to buy it. Nothing makes me crazier than seeing other small business owners complain about the unfairness of e-commerce and how no one is buying what they are selling and then I click over to their website and it has zero useful product description and all of their pictures look like it was taken on their grandmother's Afghan on their sofa at 10:30 at night under a bad yellow 60 W lightbulb. And I know you think I'm joking right now, but I promise I've seen this exact setup time and time again accompanying someone whining about the unfairness of the market. People are not going to buy things from you or take you seriously online if what you are presenting is such a total contradiction from how we are used to shopping online. I've seen the same thing, but in the opposite extreme of too much thought and effort being put into images where everything is overly cutesy or Photoshopped, or has some sort of theme with graphics in the background, while I love a good theme, and definitely have lots of images that have wooden tables, granite, fabric etc. in the background of product images. I always have white background images for the main website pages. As I had mentioned earlier, I have gone through many phases with branding and really tried to keep the brand separate from my own personal taste, or aesthetic because I know I'm not everyone's cup of tea. However, what has felt most authentic to me as far as branding goes, was really to look at it almost like I would my own personal style and getting

128

dressed. I gravitate towards maybe two neutrals and an accent. Same with fonts, two basics, and an accent, and then let it really feel like you. Repeat these themes over and over again in your images, logos, emails, etc. There really is something to be said for everything kind of matching like outfits. This is something I've really come to appreciate more in the past 10 years of my own wardrobe. I used to have lots of different tops and bottoms that I picked up out of the clearance section and figured I was cool enough to figure out how to make interesting outfits out of them, and that worked out most of the time it definitely led to decision fatigue on a regular basis. Last time, I got mad at my closet and pulled everything out and re-organized it. I followed a friend's advice. She said especially with athleisure-type outfits to actually hang them together in matching groups on the same coat hanger so I could easily pick up one basically monochromatic outfit and be about my day. You can really say the same thing for branding. I use the same email templates over and over again I have the same look and feel to my social media post so even if my brand is pink and sparkly and maximalist I feel it's at least matching and coordinated because it's consistent. Think about it even though Apple products come in a wide range of colors and models when we think of Apple branding, most of us, think of those extremely sturdy white boxes that we are afraid to throw away with the minimalist white Apple logo.

So now I know what you're thinking that's all well and good but how do you get "fans" to get on my email list to even see this great marketing? I just told you that I had given up "being popular " in certain areas online so what's the trick? In my experience, there is a lot of smoke and mirrors online. I'm not saying I'm the biggest name in any particular area but the people who resonate with me are a fantastic online community who all jive and encourage each other. Here is a little lesson I picked up from personal experience. I sell online courses on my website and while at the time of writing this, they are not the top seller from month to month but they are something I'm proud of. One day I was contacted by the owner of another fiber arts business that from my point of view was " way bigger " than my brand was. She wanted to sell courses on similar topics on her website and wanted to work with other creators in a collaboration of sorts where she would host and promote them and there was some sort of money splitting. I honestly don't remember too many of the details because it clearly didn't work out. While emailing back in forth about this plan of hers she mentioned the size of her email list as a way to I guess entice people to want to be promoted through her brand. I was really surprised because it was less than half the size of mine at the time. I was shocked because in my imagination her brand was so much larger and " more successful" than mine. As it turns it she didn't like my videos which I didn't care about because my courses match the style of my YouTube Chanel which has proven to be a success so I wasn't planning on changing. I in turn was not impressed with her marketing reach or audience because I felt that despite her brand being more popular in certain Facebook groups my brand clearly had more reach and conversion. This was an eye-opener for me that you can't always judge the successes or profitability of the brands you are comparing yourself to on social media. I don't mean any of this mean. This brand is fabulous and I'm sure performing way better than me in some areas, my takeaway was to not discount my own work despite online popularity. My website and branding, while there is always room for improvement translates as an established professional brand and that has really helped to snowball my sales and search-ability online. If you want to grow your email list you need to have some sort of an offer on your website that people will sign up to get like a coupon, e-book, special offer, etc. Then if your email platform allows you can set up a few automated emails to go out to people with info that they will genuinely find helpful and endear you to them. Another common email list fear is that if you email too much you will bother people and they will unsubscribe. You want to send out good content that people enjoy getting and that way the people who really jive with you will fall more in love with what you do and the people you aren't right for WILL unsubscribe and that way you don't end up having an email list full of people who don't like what you're about. You will end up with a healthier email list and as you grow and end up paying to send emails(by size of recipients) to people who will just mark you for spam.

To recap the tips covered in this chapter. First, you want to plot out a brand you can get behind even if it's as simple as " Designs by (your name)" or whatever. Then design a classic product line full of whatever it is that you want to be known for on a repeatable basis of services or products. After you've ironed that out you can start rotating in smaller seasonal lines to keep people excited and move them in and out with sales and promotions to your email list! That's the second part is to set up an email list with some sort of coupon offer to get people to join. Then you just keep all this going with consistent branding with quality images and content that seems natural and alluring to you. I know that seems like a lot but I promise once you get a product line and a vibe nailed down it really does all grow on itself over time. Also, keep in mind that nothing stays static forever. My brand has grown and changed so much over the years but at a gradual enough pace that it has felt mostly organic.

What do you really want?
Write down the big end goal.

Who is the person who gets
to have the life you want?
What do you need to change
or embody to be more like
that person?

What is the next right move
towards the larger goal?

Email List Checklist

What PDF, coupon, or offer can you create
to entice people to join your email list?

Checklist for Luxe Branding

- An App or website to create White background Product images (there are many).

- Pick 2-3 colors that appeal to your aesthetic: 2 neutral and one pop of color as a soft bet.

- Create a consistent style to your content and just keep posting.

- Figure out what common ground you have with the potential customers for your niche and then repeatedly make content that will appeal to them. Share their loves and frustrations.

Afterword

Mindset

Arguably the most important part

I can't really think of anything more important to tell you than mindset. I'm sitting here writing and I can tell that this is nearing the end of this particular book. I can already tell that many of these topics I'm itching to expand on in other conversations and future books. I don't want to overwhelm you with too much info at one time. I'm trying to imagine who you are reading this book. What your most immediate goals would be? I named this book "Entrepreneurial Trophy Wife" (Later Feral) as a joke but also in an effort to appeal to women who wanted to be both appreciated and free in their families as well as whatever part of the business world they choose. I think it's natural to want people to notice and appreciate our efforts in all aspects of our lives but more than that to have the freedom to fund and structure our lives the way we see fit. To me achieving a level of freedom and prosperity where you can make your own rules while having enough flexibility and happiness to really show up as the best version of yourself for the people you love is the ultimate goal.

I am proud to say that for me at least I'm in a small way already living out these dreams for myself and I'm grateful every day. That's my main reason for writing this book is in the small hope that it might help someone else get to that sweet spot in their own life. I can't tell you what exactly your dream girl experience is for your life but I can tell you that if you get clear to yourself on what that dream girl life would be and then really lean into listening to that still small voice in your head that you'll be a lot closer than you think. I personally think all women are a little magic. I think we are the energy source and powerhouse to so many people in our lives even if we don't notice. Men may always want to think they are the captain of the ship but where would they be without the constant motor of the women in their lives? We need to learn to not just inspire and motivate the people we love but more importantly use our own power to fuel our own dreams. We have so much power to pull things straight out of the ether that so many of us never even realize. Write down who and what you want your life to be, pray, or search your soul for answers on your next right step towards that. Even if it's just go take a shower and wash your face, drink more water, and learn a new skill. In my case just keep typing one more badly misspelled sentence after another. Believe it or not, it'll all string together and equal something better. Remember the more little victories you can prove to your own subconscious the more you'll start to trust yourself. Stop feeling like you're taking up too much space or being someone you're not. Everyone feels fake to an extent. Be the main character in your own life. So many people play small if you're even a little brave you'll be ahead of the pack. I think that's where I'll end this one. Just keep being a little brave. I watch my daughters in elementary school every day have to be a little brave at something new. It's easy for me to tell them to take no shit from the mean lunch lady but that's a big deal when your a little kid. Every day they try new things and keep going even if they're nervous and I know that they get some of that nerve from me. I know that they are seeing me do scary or new things and I'm still here to tell about it. You can too. Trust me.

After thoughts

Thank you for reading this book! This has been the new brave thing I've been working on for over a year now and I'm terrified and thrilled to think that anyone would have read to this point. If you want to shoot me an email you can find me at erin@feralscene.com You can find me on all the socials as either ErinSJames , FeralScene or Craftyhousewifeyarns or some combination of both. I have a prolific YouTube Channel that will have info on indie business and the fiber arts come find me for either. I also have an ever-growing collection of crafting subscriptions and online courses for fiber arts and coming soon indie business topics like this book. Let me know what you'd like to know more about. You can also find my podcast in all the places.

About the Author

Erin James is an author, indie business strategist, and the founder of Feral Scene—a brand that blends fiber arts, creative freedom, and sustainable entrepreneurship. With a background in Anthropology and Art History and years of experience in fine art sales, Erin brings a curator's eye and a cultural lens to the world of handmade business.

She's built a career helping artists and entrepreneurs stay true to themselves while building brands that are both profitable and personal. Her work bridges the gap between artistry and commerce, encouraging creatives to take up space, earn unapologetically, and define success on their own terms.

You can find her on YouTube @feralscene or on

social media as Erin.S.James

You can connect with me on:
- 🌐 https://feralscene.com
- 🔗 https://bio.site/erinjames

www.ingramcontent.com/pod-product-compliance
Lightning Source LLC
Chambersburg PA
CBHW060535130626
46553CB00002B/762

9 7 9 8 9 9 0 5 9 3 9 0 9